Reaching for the Olive Branch

UNRWA
and Peace
in the
Middle East

Milton Viorst

THE MIDDLE EAST INSTITUTE ◆ WASHINGTON, D.C.

The views expressed in this book are those of the author and not necessarily those of UNRWA, the Middle East Institute, or Indiana University Press.

The paper used in this publication meets the minimum requirements of American National Standard for Information Sciences—Permanence of Paper for Printed Library Materials, ANSI Z39.48-1984

Manufactured in the United States of America

Copyright © 1989. Milton Viorst
All rights reserved.
Viorst, Milton.
  Reaching for the olive branch : UNRWA and peace in the Middle East
  Milton Viorst.
    p. cm.
  ISBN 0-253-36256-3 (Middle East Institute : alk. paper)
  ISBN 0-253-20580-8 (Middle East Institute : pbk. : alk. paper)
  1. United Nations Relief and Works Agency for Palestine Refugees in the Near
  East. I. Title.
HV640.5.A6V56   1989   89-13487
362.87'0956—dc20   CIP

Revised edition, published for
The Middle East Institute
Washington, D.C.
by Indiana University Press
Bloomington and Indianapolis

Contents

Foreword   v

UNRWA area of operations map*

I   Intifada   1
       UNRWA field maps: Gaza Strip and
       West Bank

II   UNRWA's Response   8

III   The Early Days   32

IV   UNRWA as an Institution   47

V   In Lebanon   63
       UNRWA field map: Lebanon

VI   In Jordan   83
       UNRWA field map: Jordan

VII   In Syria   95
       UNRWA field map: Syrian Arab Republic

VIII   UNRWA in the Future   107

       Index

*Maps are taken from *UNRWA 1988*, a publication of UNRWA's Public Information Office. Note: Spellings of place names on maps may not always correspond with the text because of differences in transliteration.

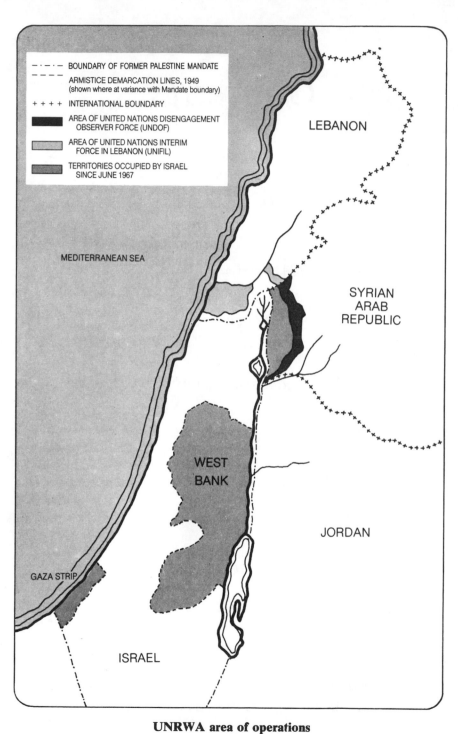

UNRWA area of operations
Not to be considered an authority on the delineation
of international boundaries

Foreword

When UNRWA was established in 1949, it was not designed as a permanent organization. Its founders hoped for an early solution to the problem of the Palestinian refugees, but that did not come about. The intervening history of UNRWA is the history of the Middle East and of the suffering of more than two million refugees who required health and education services, adequate housing, safe water supplies and sanitation systems, and who faced a host of other problems. These problems have been further aggravated not only by the passing years but also, since December 1987, by the harsh measures used to put down the uprising in the occupied territories. UNRWA, which for 40 years has sought to abate the suffering of the refugees, cannot be abolished until a solution to the problem is found. Thus, its mandate continues.

In 1983 the Middle East Institute asked Milton Viorst to do a study on UNRWA and its role in the Middle East. We published that study in 1984. This 1989 publication brings the story up to date. Why publish a new account of the organization? In the intervening six years the Middle East has undergone dramatic changes. Because new factors must be considered, we asked Mr. Viorst to bring the story into current focus. To prepare this report, he returned to the area in the spring of this year. He was accorded every courtesy by UNRWA's staff, both in the field and at its headquarters, in making its documents available and in arranging interviews. In expressing our gratitude to UNRWA for this kind assistance, we feel it is also important to note that the book represents the author's own assessment of the situation.

A book about a bureaucratic organization can be dull. That is not the case here. This is a book about people—those who need and those who give help—and about the 40-year period in which this work has gone on. It examines the dedication of the UNRWA staff and the magnitude of the day-to-day problems with which it deals. It is a book, moreover, that emphasizes in a dramatic way the need for a peace in the Middle East that will make the work of UNRWA no longer necessary. Peace, whenever it comes, will bring with it endless satisfaction to the staff of UNRWA and to the many people who seek the end of suffering and the restoration of human dignity to the inhabitants of the camps.

Lucius D. Battle
President, The Middle East Institute
October 1989

I

Intifada

In the Gaza Strip in early December of 1987, an Israeli was stabbed—not an unusual event within the perspective of 20 years of Israel's military occupation. Throughout the territories occupied in the Six-Day War of 1967, the West Bank as well as the Gaza Strip, violence was commonplace in the daily encounters of Israelis and Palestinians.

But, unlike earlier incidents, this one did not become simply a number in a column of statistics, an incremental confirmation of the horrid relations between the two peoples currently inhabiting the Holy Land. It unleashed a cataclysmic chain of events, the culmination of which—as this is written in mid-1989—is still not apparent.

When an Israeli truck two days later slammed into two cars carrying Arab workers, killing four and injuring seventeen, rumors raced through the Gaza Strip that the driver was a relative of the stabbing victim, intent on revenge. After Israeli investigators dismissed the driver of the truck with a traffic citation, young Palestinians in the Jabalya refugee camp went on a rampage of protest that rumbled irresistibly across the Gaza Strip and, from there, into the West Bank.

The Israeli army reacted with the insensitivity that

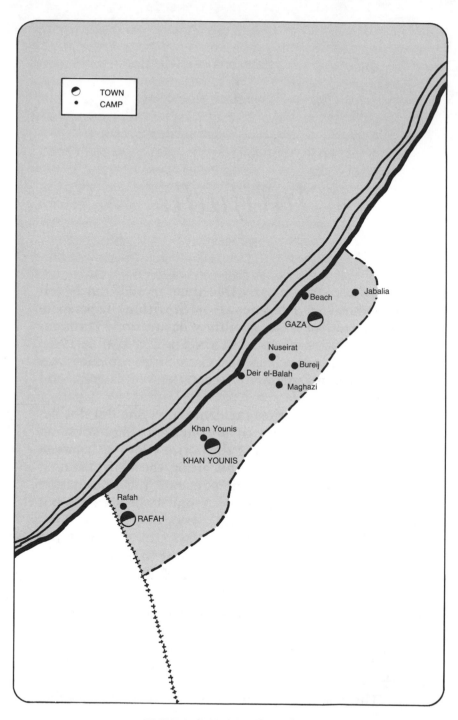

UNRWA field map: Gaza Strip
Registered refugee population in the Gaza Strip: 459,074
Proportion of total registered refugee population: 20%

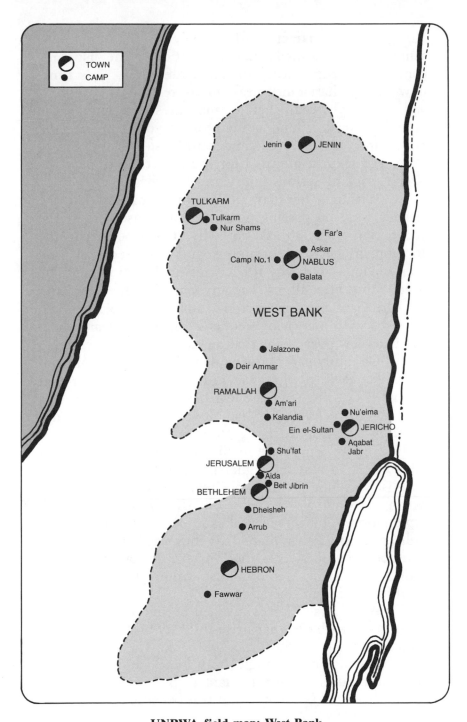

UNRWA field map: West Bank
Registered refugee population in the West Bank: 385,634
Proportion of total registered refugee population: 17%

has generally characterized its rule of the territories, sending heavily armed soldiers to put down the disorders, confident of the efficacy of harsh measures. This time, however, the harsh measures did not restore its authority, and, in fact, as steadily harsher measures were applied, the protests spread. Young women joined young men in the ranks and, in unprecedented numbers, Palestinians of every age seemed prepared for the first time to defy the Israelis, risking serious injury and even death.

Within a few days it became apparent that the clashes were no passing phenomenon. Observers of the occupation began to ask not why it had occurred—the antagonism between occupiers and occupied had long been obvious—but why it occurred at that moment. The Israeli army, after all, had been in control of the West Bank and the Gaza Strip since 1967, and though clashes had occurred with increasing frequency in recent years, there had been few overt signs that an explosion was pending.

Certainly part of the explanation lay in the unusually feisty feelings of teenagers in the territories at that moment, exulting over the feat of a Palestinian guerrilla who some weeks earlier had flown from Lebanon into Israel in a motorized hang glider and killed six Israeli soldiers on an army base in the Galilee. The message of this exploit, in which the guerrilla also died, was that the Israelis were not invulnerable to Palestinians who were willing to stand up to them. But that was a short-term explanation. A longer view takes into account the growing feelings among Palestinians that they were steadily being abandoned by outsiders—the Western powers, the Soviet Union, even their Arab brothers—whom they had hoped would secure their liberation.

When Israeli forces invaded Lebanon in 1982 with the aim of crushing what little military power the Palestinians had, the world turned its back. The Palestinians contended that not a single Arab state stepped forth to help their cause. By 1985, the Israelis had withdrawn from all but a sliver of Lebanon, but it was because the Lebanese themselves, not some outside power, had made occupation intolerable.

Meanwhile, Washington continued to proclaim that it would not support a Palestinian right to self-determination and was preparing to close the Palestine Liberation Organization's (PLO) representational offices in Washington and New York. A 1985 squabble between PLO Chairman Yasir Arafat and Jordan's King Hussein destroyed the prospect of a joint delegation to a proposed international peace conference. In the fall of 1987, the Arab heads of state, meeting in Amman, publicly placed the settlement of Palestinian claims against Israel behind an end to the Iran-Iraq war in the list of Arab priorities. Finally, the Reagan-Gorbachev summit in the first week of December came to a close without a word having been spoken about resolving the Middle East conflict. By then, Palestinians had to conclude that if they were ever to attain their freedom, they would have to do it on their own.

Israeli officials initially blamed the PLO for the disturbances spreading through the territories but, to everyone's surprise, the PLO claimed none of the credit. On the contrary, the evidence was convincing that the PLO knew no more about the uprising than what it learned over Israeli radio. After two or three weeks of relentless disorders, the Israelis were ready to admit that they faced a *popular* movement that they did not know how to control. The movement was new to Arab-Israeli relations, and the world quickly accepted the name *intifada*—meaning "shaking off"—which the Arabs gave it.

What threw the Israelis off stride was not only the commitment of the Palestinians but the tactics they adopted, more by happenstance, it seems, than by any prearranged design. These tactics fell loosely under the rubric of nonviolent protest, a doctrine that had recently been introduced to the occupied territories by Palestinians familiar with the civil rights and anti-Vietnam War movements in the United States. By the standards of Mahatma Gandhi and Martin Luther King, Jr., the intifada was never nonviolent. Transposed to the streets of the West Bank and Gaza, the tactics drawn from these thinkers should more accurately be called "nonlethal." Still, as an ongoing practice, they were vastly different from anything the Palestinians had ever before tried or anything the Israeli army had encountered.

Based on a long Middle Eastern tradition of protest by stone-throwing, these tactics shifted the onus for drawing blood in the conflict from the Palestinians to the Israelis. As these words are written, the Palestinians have suffered more than 600 dead, the Israelis about 40, but Israel's celebrated armed forces, notwithstanding the disproportion in casualties, have failed conspicuously to put down the rebellion. The Israelis never seem to know where the next protest will break out. Every refugee camp, every town and village in the West Bank and the Gaza Strip has been caught up in the momentum. Inhabitants routinely declare where they live "free villages" and raise the green, white, red, and black Palestinian flag on the public square. The occupation forces then arrive to suppress this audacity, usually arresting a few young men, only for these villages to be declared "free" again when the army leaves.

Israeli tear gas and guns have proven to be no match for rock-throwing teenagers. The Palestinians seem prepared to endure whatever casualties, detention, social distress, and economic hardship the Israelis can inflict. It is estimated that the Gross National Product (GNP) in the territories fell by at least 25 percent between the start of the intifada and mid-1989; unemployment among wage-earners was about a third. Having cut back even on its minimal services, the Israeli administration in the occupied territories lapsed into disarray. Nonetheless, morale in the West Bank and Gaza is higher than it has been in many decades and is buoyed by the sense that sympathy worldwide has shifted to the Palestinian camp.

"We are past the point of no return," one Palestinian remarked to me. "Suffering is not a limiting factor any longer." Few Palestinians believe the world will indefinitely fail to react to their struggle for freedom or that the Israeli occupation will ever again be what it was before December 1987. Meanwhile, the intifada continues.

II

UNRWA's Response

T he intifada placed the United Nations Relief and
Works Agency for Palestine Refugees in the Near East
(UNRWA) in a new situation. For nearly 40 years,
UNRWA has served the mandate bestowed on it by the
General Assembly of providing assistance to the homeless
and needy refugees (and their descendants) of the Arab-
Israeli wars. At the same time, it has tried to hold
conscientiously to the requirement of political neutrality
in the ongoing Israeli-Arab struggle.

Since the establishment of the state of Israel,
UNRWA has survived a series of emergencies: Israel's
capture of the Gaza Strip in 1956, the Six-Day War and the
occupation of the West Bank and Gaza in 1967, the
Jordanian-Palestinian battles of 1970, the Lebanese civil
war that has raged since 1975, and the Israeli invasion of
Lebanon in 1982. In each of these crises, its staff—
currently about 130 international civil servants and
18,000 locals, themselves refugees—has often been called
upon to perform under conditions of great personal jeop-
ardy. Throughout these decades, while armies repeatedly
fought, the Palestinian refugee community has been
looked upon as a victim with an interest in the outcome of
these struggles but without being a direct participant in
them. The intifada changed that.

For the first time, Palestinian refugees as a community became a central participant, both in challenging the occupation and as a target of coercive measures by the occupiers. For their resistance, the refugees were subjected, individually and collectively, to punitive measures—curfews, fines, demolition or sealing of homes and shelters, the closing of schools, incarceration without trial. In confrontations with soldiers, their young people suffered wounds from bullets, clubs, and gas, and many were wounded or gassed who were not involved at all. As a matter of daily routine, these were conditions that UNRWA had not encountered before.

The UNRWA leadership had to decide whether the agency would be a simple bystander to these conditions. It could treat its humanitarian responsibilities as if nothing had changed from the earlier days of "benign" occupation, or reinterpret its mandate to intercede between the occupying army and the refugee community in whatever measure possible; it had serious questions to consider. By offering medical care to a youngster wounded by an Israeli rifle bullet during a political demonstration, was not UNRWA helping to prolong the intifada? In bringing food into a village under curfew, was not UNRWA thwarting legitimate coercion by the occupying army to restore order? Was not such assistance political, within the meaning of its General Assembly mandate, and therefore prohibited? In examining the implication of these questions, the choice UNRWA faced was between an active and a passive interpretation of its duties. In fact, UNRWA's answer was foreordained by a tradition established in its earliest days and repeatedly reaffirmed, most dramatically in the unending chaos of Lebanon.

"It would be disingenuous to claim that UNRWA can perform its tasks without reference to politics," said Giorgio Giacomelli, UNRWA's commissioner-general. "We exist because of politics. However hard we try, we can't avoid it." Giacomelli, an Italian diplomat, has held

UNRWA's highest post since 1985, when he succeeded the retiring Olof Rydbeck, a Swede who had been commissioner-general since 1979. A tall, slim, athletic man, Giacomelli, 59 years old, had been in charge of Italy's assistance programs to the developing world prior to his joining UNRWA. His office is in Vienna, Austria, UNRWA headquarters since it was driven out of Beirut in 1978 by the Lebanese civil war. During one of his periodic tours of UNRWA's field installations, I interviewed him in the spring of 1989 in the Italian embassy in Damascus where he had once spent five years as ambassador.

"Our mission must take political reality into account," Giacomelli said. "If we are to do our work, we must remain on speaking terms with everyone concerned with the refugees, including both Israel and the PLO. Most of UNRWA's work, in our schools and clinics and offices, is done by Palestinians. We are very strict with them. 'You are entitled to your feelings,' we tell them, 'but you are not allowed to let them influence your work.' UNRWA is very careful not to take sides. I tell them to remember that we are helping people.

"Of course, we sympathize with the Palestinians. It is our mission to help them. But we can do no more than provide them with assistance. If I send a few trucks into a camp after weeks of curfew to deliver rations, I understand that in a sense it is politics. But mostly, it is humanitarian. Our relations with the Israelis are naturally strained. It is inevitable that providing humanitarian assistance clashes—the Red Cross found this out long ago—with the objectives of the people whose job it is to maintain order. I go to see Israel's leaders as often as I can. Sometimes we agree to disagree, but there is no animosity between us. They understand what we are there to do. Even if Israel sees the Palestinians as the enemy, they must be taken care of—and that's our role."

Giacomelli told me that at the beginning of the intifada, the Israelis expressed suspicion that UNRWA was serving as a conduit for money to the Palestinians. UNRWA produced its books, he said, and they were clean.

UNRWA, he said, provides financial assistance to hardship cases—the wives and children of detainees, for example—but smuggling money is not in its mandate.

"The Israelis, in discussing UNRWA's responsibilities, say routinely," Giacomelli continued, " 'Don't go beyond your mandate.' We concur but we differ with the Israelis on what the mandate is. I believe UNRWA's mandate is flexible, not explicit," Giacomelli said. "We provide the refugees with the help they need, when they need it. Once they needed tents. Now they need surgeons to fix bones broken by clubs or bullets. We haven't extended the hours of our clinics in order to encourage the uprising, but there is no use filling the shelves with aspirin or anti-polio vaccine when we know statistically that several dozen humans will be killed in demonstrations each month, and hundreds will be injured by tear gas, beatings, and bullets, whether they be high-velocity bullets or plastic bullets or rubber-coated steel bullets. Our medical responsibility must address the need that exists.

"Maybe the refugees whom we serve gain confidence from our being there, but in providing humanitarian aid I believe that we are not encouraging the intifada. The young people who take to the streets don't think of us when they throw stones. They think of their own dreams and aspirations."

In the two decades prior to the intifada, UNRWA had settled into a rather undramatic routine in the West Bank and the Gaza Strip, seeing that its clients were reasonably well housed, whether inside or outside the territories' 28 refugee camps, and that their basic health and welfare needs were served. Over the years, it had worked to make life in the camps tolerable, bringing in clean water, sewerage systems and electricity, providing for the regular pick-up of trash. Though for budgetary reasons it had eliminated the general distribution of food in 1982, it still provided rations to nearly 60,000 refugees classified as "hardship cases."

It was education, however, that took first place as UNRWA's most important responsibility as the decades passed, and by the 1987–88 academic year, the agency was providing schooling for some 40,000 pupils in 98 schools in the West Bank and nearly 90,000 pupils in 146 schools in the Gaza Strip. Two-thirds of its budget went into its classrooms and, based on test results, they offered an excellent education, superior to that of the public schools, which were run first by Egypt in Gaza and Jordan in the West Bank, and after 1967 by Israel in both. To staff these schools, UNRWA employed nearly 4,000 teachers, all refugees themselves, making the agency the single largest employer in the occupied territories and a bulwark of the local economy.

During the period after the Israeli conquest of the territories, UNRWA's relations with the military administration were often strained, not as much in the first decade when the Labor Party governed as after the electoral victory of Menachem Begin's Likud in 1977, which brought with it a significant influx of right-wing Israeli settlers. Palestinians and settlers clashed routinely in the ensuing years, and UNRWA was frequently targeted for criticism by the government for siding with the Palestinians. The Israelis nonetheless valued UNRWA, acknowledging tacitly that it performed important services which, in its absence, would fall upon the government. For the most part, both the Israelis and UNRWA understood the advantage of not letting their differences get out of hand, and as the years went by, the relationship, if never very warm, evolved into one of live-and-let-live.

Palestinians, of course, came to appreciate UNRWA even more than did Israelis, though in the early days Palestinians were sometimes suspicious that it was a tool of those whose objective it was to perpetuate their exile. Sometimes branded as ineffectual by the refugee community, it was actually a target for reproaches directed at the Western powers for failing to provide as much help as the Palestinians thought they should have and particularly for failing to help the Palestinians get back their land.

With the coming of the intifada, the tenor of criticism has changed slightly, though it has remained muted. In 1989, for the first time, I heard a refugee complain that UNRWA conspires to deny Palestinians control over their own future. "No Palestinian makes policy for UNRWA," the critic said. The observation, which was accurate enough, is the product of the same wave of pride and self-awareness, i.e., nationalism, that produced the current uprising. For now, Palestinians know they need what UNRWA does for them, but the intifada has given them a surge of confidence about what they can do for themselves.

UNRWA was apparently less surprised—at least, marginally—than the military government when the intifada broke out. In contrast to the Israelis, who had an extensive network of informers to keep them abreast of what was happening in the territories—developed through the twin weapons of intimidation and bribery—UNRWA had a rather open and trusting relationship with the local population. It was based on confidence and trust built up over four decades of involvement. The principal channel of its information was its 7,000 Palestinian employees. Informally, UNRWA's people conducted an ongoing exchange of information with the refugees in its schools and clinics and in the streets of refugee camps. UNRWA was thus better informed than the Israelis, particularly about changing moods and aspirations throughout the West Bank and Gaza.

"We were waiting for something to happen," said Robert L. Hopkins, UNRWA's field director in Jerusalem. "We were surprised only that it took so long."

Two weeks after the intifada broke out, the UN Security Council passed Resolution 605, calling upon the secretary-general to examine conditions in the territories and to recommend "ways and means for ensuring the safety and protection of the Palestinian civilians under Israeli occupation." By then, the clashes that started in Gaza had spread to every camp and to nearly every town in the two territories. Giacomelli had already protested to the Israelis over their "heavy-handed action" in suppressing demonstrations and UNRWA, having developed a flexible set of bureaucratic procedures in anticipation of trouble, had begun taking steps to provide assistance to the refugee community.

On January 21, 1988 with the intifada six weeks old, Secretary-General Javier Perez de Cuellar submitted his report to the Security Council. It was based largely on a field investigation by Marrack Goulding, the UN's undersecretary-general for political affairs. Goulding had received an icy welcome in Israel, whose government contended that the UN had no jurisdiction in the occupied territories. He was excluded by the army from two refugee camps in the Gaza Strip and harassed by military operations in others. He witnessed incidents in which curfews endangered UNRWA personnel who were evacuating the wounded or feeding the hungry. Perez de Cuellar's report noted that Shmuel Goren, Israel's coordinator in the territories, had assured Goulding that security forces had strict orders not to mistreat civilians, although Goulding repeatedly encountered evidence to the contrary.

Perez de Cuellar, in citing Israel's refusal to apply the protection of the Fourth Geneva Convention to the refugees, said the Israeli government held that the application was not required. Israel would have this obligation only if it had replaced a "legitimate sovereign" in the territories, which was true neither of Egypt in the Gaza Strip nor Jordan in the West Bank prior to 1967. In dismissing this contention, Perez de Cuellar cited contrary interpretations of the Convention's language. Nonetheless, Israel, he reported, contends that as a matter of choice it follows the "humanitarian provisions" of the Fourth Geneva Convention— though the army routinely waived them, for example, to destroy houses and deport civilians for alleged security reasons.

As for UNRWA, Perez de Cuellar urged adoption of a policy of intervention with "the occupying power to help individuals . . . resist violations of their rights (e.g., land confiscations) and to cope with the day-to-day difficulties of life under occupation, such as security restrictions, curfews, harassment, (and) bureaucratic difficulties." He also proposed enlargement of UNRWA's international staff and called for the agency to make no distinction in extending humanitarian aid between Palestinians who have refugee status and those who do not.

The secretary-general's proposals were more an endorsement of what UNRWA had already found itself doing than they were recommendations for new operations. Representing UNRWA, Giacomelli had, in fact, collaborated with Perez de Cuellar in drafting them. The resolution containing the proposals, however, was never formally adopted. It was debated in the Security Council in February 1988 and vetoed by the United States on the grounds that, on balance, it was anti-Israel. The United States raised no objections, however, to the recommendations directed specifically at UNRWA, which the agency interpreted as authority to continue its work.

The bloody character of the intifada has required UNRWA to shift the emphasis of its operations, temporarily, at least, from education to health services. These services had for many years provided the refugees with basic health care. In addition to laboratories, dental offices, maternity wards and mother-child care centers, UNRWA runs 41 health clinics that have offered a range of general medical attention to the refugees. It also operates a fleet of ambulances and subsidizes 400 beds in West Bank and Gaza hospitals. These facilities were not equal to the painful demands of the intifada, however, forcing upon UNRWA a major new effort to deal with the emergency.

At the same time, UNRWA's attention to schooling was curtailed by order of the Israeli military administration. In Gaza, the army had closed the schools sporadically, but in the West Bank the entire educational system—all of the public schools and the universities, as well as the UNRWA schools—was ordered halted soon after the conflict began. The army has not since allowed them to reopen. It has even arrested teachers for conducting extracurricular classes in their homes.[1]

UNRWA protested the Israeli order, categorizing it as punitive, and argued that, as a practical matter, school attendance gave children an outlet for their energy. The agency expressed its concern that some adolescents who were deprived of a year or two of school might be lost to education forever. The army replied that the West Bank schools were an assembly point for students coming from a wide area; Gaza, on the other hand, crowded so many people into such a small space that the schools did not play that role. Denying any punitive intent, the army said that the schoolyards of the West Bank were the beachhead on which young Palestinians organized for trouble. It said it had fewer security problems when the schools were closed. UNRWA, while regularly repeating its protests, had no choice but to comply.

Whatever its claims under international law, UNRWA understood that it could not contest the right of the Israeli government, as a prerogative of sovereignty, to have the last word in the disputes between them. What was more exasperating to the UNRWA staff than losing arguments was the arbitrariness of the process by which the army ruled.

"What is strange about the military administration," Hopkins said, "is that there seem to be no uniform directives. Often, the officers operate like free-lancers. Whoever the Israeli is on the spot seems to make the policy. The military governor in Nablus once warned us that if any UNRWA doctor in the refugee camp treated a victim of the army's action, he would impose a curfew on the entire camp. Obviously, we can't tell our doctors not to treat patients. I protested to the chief of administra-

---

[1]Under pressure from the United States, the Israeli government authorized the reopening of West Bank schools in phases, beginning with the elementary level, on July 22, 1989. The preparatory level (grades six through nine) resumed operation on August 3. The authorization applied to both UNRWA and public schools but not to universities.

tion—and there was no curfew. I never heard the order again.

"The last chief of administration for the West Bank helped solve problems. He was generally concerned with the Palestinians, in a humanitarian way. The current chief is a hard-liner, a dogmatic law-and-order man. Communicating with him is like pouring water into sand. Letters and calls go unanswered. Talking with him gets nowhere. But he's the man who makes the rules, and we have to deal with him every day."

Zacharias Backer, Hopkins' counterpart in the Gaza Strip, expressed almost identical complaints. Backer retired in 1988 as a regimental commander in the Norwegian army to accept the UNRWA post. A tall spare man, 59 years old, he replaced Bernard Mills, a retired major in Britain's special forces, whose outspokenness had made him the vortex of controversy between UNRWA and the Israelis. Mills, having long worked alongside Arabs, apparently lost his restraint in responding to Israeli excesses in the suppression of the intifada. Though never precisely told to leave, Mills was said to be a marked man after he challenged the truthfulness of an assertion by Israeli Defense Minister Yitzhak Rabin that the army did not use live ammunition in confrontations with the rock-throwers. Backer's opinion of the conduct of Israeli troops was hardly more favorable than Mills', but he has been somewhat more discreet in manifesting his concern.

Backer told me when we talked in the spring of 1989 in his Gaza office that he thought the lines of command in the Israeli army were tangled, leaving too much power of decision in the hands of noncommissioned and junior officers. He commended the restraint of Israel's older reservists, while condemning the conduct of the elite units, particularly the much heralded Givati Brigade, four of whose soldiers were court-martialed for abuses shortly after we met.

"The reservists are older and more mature," Backer said. "They don't look for trouble. Some of the younger troops misunderstand their task, which is to calm the situation and restore peace. The elite forces simply don't know how to stand idle. If there is no business, they create it." Backer said that in Gaza demonstrations had too often gone out of control, with Palestinian teenagers provoking the soldiers, but with soldiers often provoking them back. The Israeli army has sometimes had to confine its own soldiers to their barracks, he said, in order to regain a semblance of authority over them.

It is the casualties of the intifada that have fundamentally changed UNRWA's role in the occupied territories. It has transformed UNRWA's health clinics, heretofore absorbed by prenatal care and inoculations and the common cold, into casualty treatment centers. Israel has continued to admit to its hospitals—against payment by UNRWA or Israeli health insurance—some refugees who require standard, noncombat treatment, though many fewer than before. Casualties of the fighting, however, have sometimes been denied Israeli hospital care, and many who are wounded have been reluctant to seek treatment for fear of retaliation against themselves or their families. Often the victims are the very young or the very old, injured by beatings, gassing, or gunshot, with the bullets described as rubber, plastic, or steel. Mass symptoms from tear gas—convulsions, suffocation, and miscarriages—have themselves been enough on many occasions to fill a good-sized hospital. This situation created a gap in the health-care system that UNRWA alone was available to fill. So while its classrooms stood empty, the agency turned its attention to battlefield medicine.

UNRWA hired 15 more doctors and 15 nurses from among the local pool of unemployed Palestinian doctors who had been trained in the United States, Europe, the Soviet Union, or the Arab world. It extended the hours of its clinics into early evening, particularly those located near recurring trouble spots, and it has opened up stark emergency clinics in trailers equipped with only the barest necessities but essential in periods of high casualties. When needed, it has maintained medical staffs on a 24-hour basis. It has purchased more ambulances and placed them on round-the-clock alert, moving them back and forth as needed between the West Bank and Gaza. It has enlarged its stocks of anesthetics, antibiotics, suture materials, oxygen cylinders, and plaster of Paris and bought new equipment for surgery, intensive care, and physiotherapy.

Recognizing the disruptive impact of the intifada on community life, UNRWA has also expanded its feeding programs, normally limited to preschool children, to cover youngsters up to the age of 10, pregnant and nursing women, and newborns. It has, in addition, expanded a program to distribute blankets, clothing, and cash to needy families and to repair and rebuild shelters damaged in the course of the conflict. Fortunately for UNRWA, the intifada captured worldwide attention and sympathy, and many governments responded with donations to cover the costs of the special operations.

UNRWA's budget—currently more than $200 million, coming almost exclusively from voluntary contributions of UN members—has always been stringent, leaving only the narrowest of margins for emergencies. For political reasons, the agency did not have the option of economizing by cutting services in its other areas of operation in Lebanon, Syria, and Jordan. It saved a little after the intifada started by delaying infrastructure projects in West Bank and Gaza refugee camps, but education expenses did not decline even though the schools were closed. To be ready if the army suddenly reversed its closure orders, UNRWA kept its teachers on full salary, on call to return to the classroom at a moment's notice.

In the first fiscal year of the uprising, UNRWA received more than $40 million in supplementary gifts from the international community for emergency projects in the West Bank and the Gaza Strip. Major contributions, the bulk of them designated for food and medicines, came from Canada, Denmark, Iraq, Italy, Japan, Kuwait, Libya, Morocco, the Netherlands, Norway, Qatar, Sweden, the United Arab Emirates, the United States, West Germany, and the European Community. Money also came from the

United Nation's Children's Fund (UNICEF) budget for physiotherapists and equipment to provide rehabilitative treatment to the victims of beatings and wounds, chiefly the young. UNICEF also provided training in rehabilitation for UNRWA staff members.

If UNRWA's principal and most costly response to the intifada has been in the field of medicine, its most innovative was in the area that academics now designate "conflict resolution." In the early days of the strife, the agency recognized an obligation to take special measures to keep down the level of bloodshed. An opportunity seemed to lie in the credibility that UNRWA had established with both sides. Any services it might perform as a mediator held the potential of saving lives. No other available institution was fitted to perform such a service.

UNRWA started by assigning members of its international staff—that is, the international civil servants on its payroll—to be conspicuously placed observers at trouble spots. The assumption behind the move was that their presence alone would serve as a restraint upon both sides. The agency then authorized these observers, if the circumstances held any promise, to act as negotiators in threatening situations and to deal with the Israeli army on the scene rather than pass through formal administrative channels. Gradually, the scope of the job grew, with UNRWA encouraging creativity, initiative, and judgment in the hope of narrowing the limits of violence.

At first, UNRWA observers had no title attached to their functions. Around the regional offices in Jerusalem and Gaza they came to be referred to informally as "trouble-shooters" or even "Rambos." UNRWA administrators disliked these designations, if only because the responsibility of the job was quite the opposite of what the terms suggested. UNRWA headquarters in Vienna, furthermore, became apprehensive that the press would seize upon what were essentially slang expressions and thereby distort the purpose of the mission. As a result it invented the innocuous title "Refugee Affairs Officer" and required that, even in casual conversation, the old slang terms be dropped. Since then, the job has become steadily more central to UNRWA's work in the territories and the acronym RAO has become common usage in referring to its holders.

UNRWA currently has 12 RAOs in the West Bank and 8 in the Gaza Strip. Their nationalities are American, Australian, Austrian, British, Canadian, Danish, Dutch, German, Italian, and Swedish. The first class of RAOs that UNRWA selected was composed chiefly of men of some strength and bulk. Now, several RAOs are women. All were hired in Vienna after rigorous interviews that tested them not for any specific skills but for common sense, high energy, tenacity, tact, and a capacity for staying cool in conditions of extreme tension.

John Griffith, a 41-year-old Briton with greying hair, became an RAO on the West Bank in April 1989 after working in shipping for 21 years in the Middle East. Griffith told me he had applied to UNRWA for a transportation job and, though he had no military or police training, was intrigued when he learned an RAO post was open. All he knew about it came from the description of one of the first RAOs, whom he ran into by chance in Vienna, but he liked the idea, he said, of work in which he set his own guidelines.

"Even now, I can't be too precise about what we do," Griffith told me. "Each situation in a confrontation has its own character. Each area is different. Each Israeli soldier is unique. We devise our plans as we go along. At first, the Palestinians had no idea what to make of us. By disposition, they are suspicious of anyone who noses around and asks questions. We did a lot of walking and driving around the camps, waving and smiling, to make our faces known. I still do that. But now I think they know who we are and appreciate us."

Griffith let me join him on one of his daily visits to the Jalazun camp, north of Ramallah, where swarms of smiling children, rather healthy looking but with dirty faces and tattered clothes, waved as we drove by. We stopped at several homes to talk to families who described middle-of-the-night visits by soldiers and, more frightening, by bands of settlers. Nearly all had a husband or brother in detention in Qetzi'ot, the Israeli camp in the Negev desert. The detention of thousands of wage-earners had left the community in worsening economic stress, yet the women at each house stayed faithful to Arab tradition by serving us heavy, black coffee. On many blocks of the camp lay the rubble of demolished houses. Nearly every wall was marked with graffiti whose slogans were translated to me as "Palestine is free" and "Long live the intifada."

Characteristically, the RAOs assemble about eight o'clock each morning, both in Jerusalem and in Gaza, for a meeting chaired by the director or deputy-director of UNRWA's local office. Also likely to be present are UNRWA's local legal officer and communications officer. The principal items on the agenda are the accounts the RAOs give of their experiences of the previous day along with reports acquired second-hand of events they personally missed—a skirmish between teenagers and settlers, a house demolished in a camp, a refugee hospitalized by gunshot wounds, a night-time arrest by a squad of soldiers. They also report, based on their conversations with Palestinians in the camps and towns, where trouble seems likely to occur in the upcoming 24 hours.

The director may then disclose information or admonitions imparted to him the previous day in talks with Israeli military headquarters. The communications officer might discuss how to correct some radio problem. It is the assignment of the legal officer to investigate every known clash between Palestinians and Israelis, to measure the extent of wounds and injuries, and to file formal protests with the military administration if there has been some irregularity in conduct.

The legal officer collects from the RAOs the "daily status report" that each fills out—a record of injuries and deaths, arrests and releases, confrontations and curfews, as well as damage to UNRWA installations—for every stop in the assigned itinerary. He might ask a few questions of the RAOs to supplement the reports or schedule a fuller interrogation for later in the day. When the legal officer has compiled the data he needs, he forwards it to headquarters in Vienna for the permanent file. The meetings rarely last more than 45 minutes or an hour, by which time the RAOs whom I saw were impatient to get into their cars to begin touring whatever sector of the West Bank or the Gaza Strip was assigned to them for that day.

The principal task of the RAOs is to cruise the thoroughfares of the occupied territories, showing the flag of the United Nations, keeping their eyes open for incidents, trying to forestall trouble. One RAO told me he logs about 1,500 miles a week at the wheel. The RAOs wear no uniforms or other special identification. They carry neither weapons nor gas masks. (The prescribed technique for dealing with tear gas—said to be a slight palliative, at best—is to run to the car and turn on the air-conditioning.) They are in constant radio contact with headquarters and, through the radio, with one another, ready to speed off to the main square of another camp or another town where they might be needed to file the sharp edges off some confrontation. In fact, for reasons of personal security, RAOs are in radio contact with the local headquarters 24-hours-a-day, using walkie-talkies. They do not often work nights, however, because trouble in the territories tends to diminish after dark. The assignments of the RAOs usually expire after six months (with possible six-month extensions), when they are relieved, because it is assumed that by then they will have burned out.

The RAO's first stop upon reaching a refugee camp is normally at the office of the camp services officer to check on what has transpired since last they met, usually the previous day. The camp services officer is himself a Palestinian refugee, and he is paid to keep an eye on UNRWA installations within the camp—schools, clinics, recreational centers, warehouses, and food distribution points. He supervises the water supply systems, the feeding programs and the sanitation facilities. He consults on plans for camp improvements and monitors UNRWA's diverse services, such as hospital care and scholarships. In short, the camp services officer is UNRWA's principal set of eyes and ears, and when the RAO arrives on the scene, he reports any incidents that occurred the previous night, directing the RAO to eyewitnesses whom he normally will question for the report that later goes to Vienna.

The camp services officer used to be called "camp leader," which UNRWA decided some years ago was a misnomer. At best, the camp services officer is a caretaker who in the past rarely performed much of a leadership function at all. Since the intifada, some leadership responsibilities have been thrust upon him by the nature of events. More often, however, he is caught uncomfortably between protesters and soldiers, with both turning to him for support or information. Not surprisingly, all too often he fails them both, only to be denounced from all sides for his inadequacy.

Before the intifada, leadership in the camps was exercised more or less formally by the *mukhtars*, the village elders. For many of them, their legitimacy dated back to the Palestinian villages from which they and their neighbors fled in the war of 1948. Installed in authority in the camps, the mukhtars offered advice, resolved disputes, dispensed justice, and kept the social structure intact. But it is generally agreed that over the years they were also corrupted by bribery and favors. Some had actually been selected by the military government and would move about the camps surrounded by gun-toting bodyguards. Institutionally, the mukhtars became the hub of an informer system run by the occupation authorities who used it skillfully in the interests of the status quo.

If the intifada is an uprising against the occupation, it is also a revolution against the mukhtars, and, though relatively little is known about the process, it is apparent that power has shifted to a far more daring generation—conventionally called *shebab*—much of it still in adolescence. "My kids blame me," one middle-aged Palestinian father told me, "and accuse our generation of neglecting its duties toward our people, our country, our religion. It is true that all I wanted was peace and quiet, so I could pursue my career. They say there is no point to a career without a state. I sent my older children to universities in England to keep them out of trouble but the younger ones won't go. My son served eighteen days in administrative detention, without charges, when he was sixteen. Now all he wants to do is fight. They're just not afraid of the Israelis the way we are." Not simply are the boys stronger than their fathers, my Palestinian friend told me, but the girls are stronger than both their fathers and mothers. These are the shebab who, as nearly as one can tell, run the intifada.

The military government has found it hard to accept the fact that its system of control has crumbled, and indeed it has continued to pursue its efforts at subversion with some successes. It played the followers of the PLO against the Islamic Resistance Movement (HAMAS), but the rivalry thus spawned seems only to have intensified the protests of both. It has tried to protect Palestinians who have served Israel, but the ruthless execution of some 50 so-called collaborators suggests that it has failed. Who gave the orders to kill the collaborators and who carried them out is not clear, but the murders bear witness to the awesome power exercised by the new leadership structure in the occupied territories.

Whether, and how much, this new structure is beholden to the PLO in Tunis is widely debated. Most high-level decisions relating to the intifada seem to be reached by a consensus of factions called the "unified leadership" or "unified national command." Its composition is said to be a coalition of factions that mirrors Palestinian politics on the outside. By mid-1989, there were signs that countless arrests had weakened the structure and that factionalism was on the rise. There were reports of heated debate between those who insisted that only violence would persuade Israel to give ground and those who wanted to stick with the tactics of nonlethal confrontation. Divided as it may be, however, this leadership structure persists, encouraging the rebels, frustrating the Israelis.

Inside the camps, meanwhile, the governing structure appears to be different and more local. There, underground organizations of shebab—often girls as well as boys, all born since the start of the occupation two decades ago—have succeeded to power. These teenagers are contemptuous of the mukhtars and frequently defiant toward UNRWA's camp services officers. They may or may not be loyal to a faction in the Palestinian political spectrum, but they do not forget that their principal foe remains the army of occupation.

The shebab are a major source of information for the RAOs, often tipping them off on when and where a demonstration is to take place. It is a rule of thumb that, to protect UNRWA's neutrality, the RAO's wait until they are contacted, never seeking out the refugee leadership and never asking for names or other identification. Israeli soldiers are convinced that the teenagers notify the RAOs, then wait for their arrival to start their protests, knowing the UN presence will give them protection. The army looks upon RAOs with suspicion, claiming they make the shebab bolder. The soldiers dislike the constraints imposed on their freedom to rough up the demonstrators and they grumble when injured Palestinians are rushed off to a hospital in an RAO's car. To be sure, army units, usually reservists, occasionally make deals with an RAO to defuse some particularly dicey situation, but, characteristically, the soldiers resent the RAOs whom they see as siding with the Palestinians. Though no incidents of actual violence are on record, there have been plenty of tense confrontations between RAOs and soldiers.

UNRWA authorizes its RAOs to intervene in dangerous situations, but not to interfere directly with the operations of the Israeli army and certainly not to get involved in actual combat. Sometimes, however, the line between these functions is very fuzzy. RAOs have found that to calm a volatile situation, it often is enough to sit in their cars, watching sternly. But they are also trained to park in a manner that permits a quick getaway and to stay out of the line of fire, whether of stones or bullets, when they are in the presence of fighting. So far, one RAO has been grazed by a bullet and several have been hit by stones, but none has been seriously hurt.

One morning I went off to Shufat Camp with Karin Jahr, a German woman in her thirties who had been the first female RAO in Gaza. Trained as a lawyer, Jahr had recently been transferred from Gaza to the West Bank where she was still learning the terrain. She told me that when UNRWA decided to adopt the UN's commitment to equal opportunity by hiring women as RAOs, she had applied as a way of getting away from desk work at home. Giacomelli, the commissioner-general, had pushed hard for women RAOs, in part because it was consistent with the UN's pro-feminist policy. To promote the policy, he had also opened more places for women refugees in UNRWA's vocational training centers where, except for teaching courses, men have been in a majority by a ratio of five to one. Giacomelli was also convinced that, in day-to-day contact with the intifada, women would provide UNRWA with a "gentler" touch, which would have practical value. The exposure of Palestinians to women in positions of authority was at odds with local custom, but UNRWA plunged forward. It was a "Western" decision, Jahr said, and UNRWA admitted at the start that it was unsure of the outcome.

Women RAOs first had to overcome the prejudices of the Palestinian community, she said, particularly in Gaza which is more traditional than the West Bank and where personal contact, because of the concentration of population, was more intense. Jahr said that UNRWA's women took pains to be respectful of the culture, particularly in dress, and, gradually winning the Palestinians' confidence, wound up enriching their esteem for women.

At the same time, women RAOs had fewer tense encounters with Israeli soldiers, who seemed to find them less threatening than the men and were readier to listen when they spoke; as a result, these women became quite good at abating the everyday dangers of the intifada. Finally, she said, the women gained the approval of their own male colleagues, who had shared the worries of American policemen that females in their ranks would be unable to hold their own. In contrast to these apprehensions, she insisted, women RAOs brought an unanticipated calm and composure to their work and showed a similar level of courage as the men.

Jahr and I went as observers to the distribution of food parcels in Shufat, a camp inside the Israeli-drawn boundaries of Jerusalem. In the early days of the intifada, most refugees refused food aid, apparently responding to instructions from their leadership to demonstrate their independence. For months, however, Palestinians had been living under deteriorating economic conditions, and the hardship was growing palpable.

Shufat's problem was that, unlike most camps, it is not the reconstitution of a village or a series of villages but a collection of displaced slum-dwellers from Jerusalem's Old City, particularly from the Jewish Quarter. One of the oddities of the occupation is that, because Shufat is inside the city line, the government considers it legally in Israel and, alone among the West Bank camps, its schools remained open while all others were closed. Shufat is known, among Palestinians as well as Israelis, as a tough, undisciplined place, a market of drugs and prostitution, with no recognized hierarchy of leaders to maintain order. When UNRWA received a shipment of prepackaged food items—flour, meat, sugar, rice, cooking oil—from a foreign donor, it seemed like an opportunity to relieve the distress of Shufat residents, but the agency's directors in Jerusalem were apprehensive about the distribution procedures. With misgivings, the agency finally decided to give distribution a try.

Two UNRWA trucks had preceded our arrival. One was backed up to the platform of a warehouse at the door of which refugees were already squabbling over places in line. Most of the women wore traditional Palestinian dress, colorful street-length gowns with elaborate embroidery on the chest; the men were all in work clothes. Hordes of little children milled about enjoying the activity. An UNRWA employee worked at passing out the food packages, a process slowed to a snail's pace by his checking of credentials to make sure that each family received only one, and as the minutes went by the crowd became increasingly unruly. In nearly an hour, only a dozen or so of the 1,200 available parcels had been distributed, and suddenly I saw the driver slam shut the tailgate of his truck and, followed by the second truck, drive away. UNRWA had not given the order to halt the distribution. In fact, in the confusion, no one knew who did. By then, hundreds of men and women stood around shouting and pointing fingers at one another, and the entire camp seemed to be in a surly mood. I saw no sign of violence or destruction, however, and when 10 minutes later two Israeli police vans sped through the camp gate, sirens blaring, their windows covered with wire mesh, I wondered why they were there.

The presence of the police, however, was enough to inspire a class of teenagers on a recess break at a school on the hill that overlooked the square; they proceeded to pelt the vans with stones. Some younger children who had been playing in the square changed games and pushed rocks the size of basketballs into the street, blocking the exit route from the camp. Meanwhile, from within the crowd which was now united in resistance to the Israeli presence, a din of whistles was directed mockingly at the police, who then lost their patience and fired tear gas. This action promptly dispersed the onlookers in the square, while the teenagers on the hill, recess over, retreated back to class. Their departure left Shufat quiet once again.

In the hour or so that followed, Jahr was joined by several other RAOs, and together they questioned a dozen witnesses to try to make sense of the episode. The camp services officer, who had the reputation at UNRWA headquarters of being neither strong nor reliable, should have been able to provide some insight into whether the disorders at the warehouse were spontaneous or deliberate, but it was he who had devised the distribution procedures and he pretended not to know why they had gone amiss; in addition, neither could he nor anyone else be sure who gave the orders for the trucks to take off. Were the shebab, the mukhtars, or the Israeli collaborators responsible for the fiasco? All might have had their motives but, in the end, no one had an answer.

The presence of RAOs might have prevented a more serious clash between refugees and police, which was the good news, but the bad news was that Shufat went unfed. The cause of this failure went down in the permanent record in Vienna as unknown—another mystifying episode, so to speak, in the long history of East-meets-West encounters.

Later that same morning, I went off to look at the Qalandiyya refugee camp just north of Jerusalem with Tony Charters, a 39-year-old RAO from Ireland. Charters, who arrived in Gaza in 1981 to work with relief organizations, told me that by 1987 he was fed up with the passivity of the Palestinians and had to leave. When he heard about the intifada, he said, he wanted to return, and UNRWA hired him as an RAO on the West Bank. Charters had stopped by Qalandiyya earlier that morning and obviously was aware that something was brewing. The newspapers had reported demonstrations the previous two or three days as well as the arrest of several young children. Charters directed the car through the dusty streets of the camp—home, according to UNRWA records, of 5,000 refugees—and pulled up at an intersection where the first thing I saw, some 20 yards away, was an Israeli soldier standing next to his jeep, examining the identification card (ID) of a Palestinian teenager. When the soldier saw the UNRWA car, he handed the young man his papers and sent him on his way. Charters remarked that without UNRWA's presence the soldier might have smacked the Palestinian around before returning the ID, or he might have kept it and forced the young man to pick it up at army headquarters in Beth-El, some 20 kilometers away.

Then, from the other direction, I saw the approach of a band of a dozen children ranging in age from about nine to thirteen. As the soldier's jeep drove away, they threw stones, then leaped into doorways or behind parked cars for cover. Their range was far short of the jeep and the stones fell harmlessly to the ground, but four soldiers nonetheless embarked in desultory pursuit. The problem was that in their heavy coats, wearing gloves and helmets and carrying rifles, they were no match for the children in their jeans and sweaters. As the soldiers plodded along, the children danced tauntingly away, laughing wildly, waving Palestinian flags, flinging an occasional stone that hit nothing.

Charters and I followed this contest for about half-an-hour, while from the roof of a nearby building two Israeli soldiers used binoculars to keep an eye both on the children and on us. On the street, Arab women dressed in their native gowns shuffled back and forth, carrying laundry or groceries, paying no attention to the fracas at all. Finally, the pursuing soldiers grew frustrated, climbed back into the jeep and drove away, putting an end to an encounter that was essentially innocuous, but which seemed to me like an allegory on the nature of the intifada.

III

UNRWA in the Early Days

I n the years of World War II and afterward, the Arabs of Palestine were among millions of men and women, on several continents, who were made homeless by convulsive political change. The UN's response to the overall problem was to organize an International Relief Organization, later to become the UN High Commissioner for Refugees, to see to the protection, the decent treatment, and, in most cases, the resettlement of the dispossessed in homes outside their native lands. It was a relatively small agency which achieved its humanitarian aims through steps once removed from its own action—largely by negotiation with interested governments and arrangement with voluntary agencies.

In contrast, the UN singled out the Palestinians by choosing to take responsibility for them directly. It was by no means indifferent to the benevolence extended to the refugees by public and private bodies. On the contrary, UNRWA from the start has been financed by voluntary contributions, chiefly by member states. But the General Assembly mandated UNRWA to be an "operational" agency, to provide directly the necessary services to refugees in its charge.

An explanation of this special treatment is not hard to find. In 1947, responding to the wartime decimation of European Jewry, the UN had voted to partition Palestine, creating the state of Israel for the survivors of the Holocaust and leaving the remainder as a state for the Palestinians. The Arabs rejected the UN's decision. In 1948, in the first of a series of Israeli-Arab wars, Jordan and Egypt occupied most of the land designated by the UN for the Palestinian state while Israel occupied the rest. In the course of the war, hundreds of thousands of Palestinians fled or were chased from their homes in what is now Israel. The magnitude of the exodus was at first unclear. Nonetheless, the UN reasoned it could not do less for the Palestinians than it had done for the Jews.

The tenor of the UN's reaction to the flight of the Palestinians was set by Count Folke Bernadotte, a stern Swedish nobleman named mediator of the 1948 war. Bernadotte contended that the UN had not only an obligation to provide relief to the refugees but also a duty to assure their return to their homes. "It would be an offence against the principles of elemental justice," Bernadotte told the General Assembly, "if these innocent victims of the conflict . . . who have been rooted in the land for centuries . . . were denied the right to return to their homes while Jewish immigrants flow into Palestine . . . ." Bernadotte's assassination by Jewish extremists in December 1948, far from weakening this position, served in international circles to give weight to Bernadotte's arguments.

A few weeks after Bernadotte's death, the General Assembly voted to provide for the economic relief of the Palestinian refugees, but it went a major step further in making a promise to the Palestinians that it made to no other refugee group. In paragraph II of Resolution 194 (III), the UN—by proclaiming for the dispossessed a right of repatriation or compensation—fixed the terms of the international debate that has surrounded the Palestinian refugees ever since.

In those days, the UN could hardly have been considered hostile to Israel, a reputation it has since acquired. With the same membership, the UN had earlier voted to establish the Jewish state. It is probably correct to say that a humanitarian impulse at the UN, into which was fused a postwar sense of guilt, was at the source of the vote for Israel, superseding normal considerations of practical politics. These same feelings were present in the vote for the Palestinians.

Yet the vote on the refugees was cast with little regard for what was the commanding political and social reality of the region. The UN, having the year before provided the legal basis for the realization of the Zionist dream, proceeded to legitimize the Palestinian dream. But how could the Palestinians be invited to return to an Israel whose existence they would not acknowledge and with which they were at war? Neither side was prepared at this stage to compromise in any significant way with the other's aspirations. In such circumstances, it was clear that Israeli and Palestinian dreams were in fundamental ways incompatible.

Paragraph 11 of the General Assembly resolution declared "that the refugees wishing to return to their homes and live at peace with their neighbors should be permitted to do so at the earliest practicable date. . . . " It proceeded to add that "compensation should be paid for the property of those *choosing not to return.*" (Emphasis added.)

In asserting a principle of compensation, the UN wisely provided for an alternative to repatriation, but it assigned the choice of repatriation or compensation to the refugees alone. The resolution left Israel, after winning a war to validate the UN's vote on its statehood, no say in a matter that it regarded as crucial to its future. The resolution, at least as the Israelis saw it, seemed to reward those who had contested the UN vote on the battlefield and lost.

Nonetheless, there were negotiations, of which no Palestinians were a part. It is usually forgotten that, during the year after the Israeli war of independence, Israel and the neighboring Arab states engaged in a promising series of talks to settle their relations. By mid-1949, the Israelis had agreed in principle to the repatriation of 100,000 refugees, the Jordanians and Syrians to the accommodation of the non-repatriated refugees within their borders. All parties surrounded their positions with conditions, but chief among them was Israel's reading of the requirement that the refugees consent to "live at peace with their neighbors." The Israelis interpreted the clause as meaning that establishment of an Arab-Israeli peace agreement was a prerequisite to repatriation. When the Arabs rejected a formal peace, the hopes for a resolution of the refugee problem came to an end, never again to be revived.

Meanwhile, the UN's refugee count was rising. It included, at the start, some 45,000 Jews, most of them displaced from settlements in the West Bank, which had been taken over by Jordan. The Israeli government, promptly assumed responsibility for these refugees. In contrast, no one took responsibility for the Palestinians. The Arab governments did no more than set aside land for camps where refugees were crowded together in tents, living in squalid conditions. Many were hungry.

As a stopgap measure to deal with the distress, the General Assembly acted under the power granted to it under the UN Charter to "establish such subsidiary organs as it deems necessary to the performance of its functions." In November 1948, it voted into existence a program called United Nations Relief for Palestinian Refugees (UNRPR). Without an operating staff of its own, its secretariat asked member governments to make voluntary contributions. The governments of the Arab states in which the refugees had sought asylum—themselves poorly organized, while holding the UN culpable for the problem—were far from cooperative. Work was done at its request on a voluntary basis by the Red Cross, several religious societies, and the American Friends Service Committee. Under UNRPR's ministry, supplies began arriving in the Middle East early in 1949; refugees and non-refugees alike lined up to receive them.

By June of 1949, the relief rolls had risen to nearly a million, and the voluntary agencies were swamped. It was clear by now that the UN's improvisation was not equal to the task, and at the end of 1949, UNRPR's concept was superseded in the organization known as UNRWA.

To understand the General Assembly's outlook at that time, it is important to note that next to the "R" for "relief" in the new agency's acronym was a "W," which stood for "works." The "W" distinguished UNRWA from UNRPR, which had only the "R." In the mind of the Western nations, at least, was the successful experience of the Marshall Plan, which helped, through productive investment, to restore prosperity to Europe immediately after World War II. Responding to recommendations of an economic survey mission sent by the UN to the Middle East, UNRWA was assigned the task of promoting public works to provide permanent employment to the refugees.

The General Assembly seemed not to notice an inherent contradiction between this mission, which consisted of the UN's sponsorship of an economic development program, and the UN's commitment to the refugees' repatriation. Economic development meant long-term planning wherever Palestinians had found refuge, which was quite at odds with their prompt return home. This was late 1949, however, when Israel talked of taking back a substantial segment of the refugee population and the Arabs seemed reconciled to settling the rest. The two sides appeared resigned to a solution, however imperfect. Both, in fact, voted in favor of establishing UNRWA and endorsed its program.

UNRWA's plan was to create 100,000 jobs by mid-1951, which would remove 400,000 persons, counting dependents, from the relief rolls. It commissioned designs for irrigation, forestation, and road-building projects, which in hindsight strains credulity but which for that brief moment was treated as reality. In its first year,

UNRWA actually organized road-building and reforestation programs, which employed at their peak 12,000 men. A study made at the time showed that the cost was five times more to the agency to keep a refugee at work than on relief, but in those days the international community seemed willing to pay the price.

In late 1950, the General Assembly established a Reintegration Fund of $30 million to be made available to governments of the Middle East for development projects. A year later, UNRWA recommended adding $200 million more to the fund, arguing that within two or three years relatively few refugees would still be dependent and its own services would no longer be necessary. The General Assembly, in fact, formally instructed UNRWA to prepare plans to dissolve itself without ado, turning over any residual functions to the Arab states.

Of the money in the Reintegration Fund, only $7 million was ever spent. One reason was the absence of the necessary expertise among the Arabs of that period in identifying and organizing productive projects. Another was the political service that the presence of the refugee issue on the international agenda rendered to Israel's enemies. The principal obstacle, however, was the resistance of the refugees themselves. On a practical level, the UNRWA plan looked risky to the refugees. The UNRWA ration card already guaranteed them food and a roof, schools for their children, and medical care. It was a foolproof system of economic security for which employment on uncertain UNRWA-financed projects was no substitute.

More than that, the refugees took UNRWA's large-scale development plans to mean permanent resettlement away from home, regardless of any economic advantage they might in time provide. The plans signaled a repudiation of the UN's promise of repatriation. With this consideration uppermost in the minds of the refugees, it was hard to imagine launching an economic development program much less dissolving the relief agency. Neither UNRWA nor the Arab governments were prepared to take on the challenge of overcoming the resistance of the Palestinians, the very people whom the program was supposed to help.

Explaining the abandonment of the works projects, UNRWA's director reported in 1955, "The outstanding factor which continues to condition refugee attitudes and to influence the policies of Near Eastern governments . . . is the strong desire of the refugees to return to their homeland. This feeling has not diminished . . . and its strength should not be underestimated." Without the opportunity to return to their homes—unless agreement is reached on compensation or some other political resolution of the question—"the unrequited demands of repatriation," he wrote, "will continue to be an obstacle to the accomplishment of the objective of reintegration and self-support."

The "works" proposal was finally laid to rest in 1959, after the United States, UNRWA's principal donor, called on Secretary-General Dag Hammarskjold to undertake a new study to determine whether a program of capital investment that promised to produce jobs could, in time, make the services of the agency unnecessary.

Hammarskjold conducted the study over the objections of the Arab delegations. In presenting it to the General Assembly, he based his conclusions on the central observation that "the unemployed population represented by the Palestine refugees should be regarded not as a liability but, more justly, as an asset for the future; it is a reservoir of manpower which in the desirable general economic development will assist in the creation of higher standards for the whole population of the area." Hammarskjold expressed his strong belief that prosperity, by permitting the political integration of the refugees into the existing Arab states, held out the prospect of ending the Middle East conflict.

That was not how the Arab governments conceived of ending the Middle East conflict. In a reply to the secretary-general, the representatives of ten Arab nations argued that, in focusing on economics, the study was based on a flawed premise: "The refugee problem is not an economic one . . . ," the Arabs contended. "The problem resulted directly from Zionist terrorism and from the policy of the United Nations which led to the creation of Israel. . . . The United Nations bears the full responsibility for all the deprivation, misery and hardship suffered by the refugees during all these years. It follows that the responsibility of the United Nations, and especially the responsibility of those States that had greatly influenced the course of the Palestine problem, must continue until the United Nations can take the necessary measures for the implementations of its resolution providing for the return of the refugees . . . ." By making clear that investments intended to alleviate the condition of the refugees would not be welcome in their countries, the Arab delegates dismissed once and for all any attempts at resolving the problem of the Palestinians through economic means.

It is impossible to say whether the Palestinian attitude would have developed differently had the General Assembly taken a more stern position on UNRWA's responsibilities. It is no less subject to speculation how the Arab world would have responded had there been no UNRWA at all. Certainly, there is an argument to be made that overall, UNRWA has not played a positive role. Until the intifada, some Palestinians complained that UNRWA's largesse took the fight out of the refugees, while many Israelis said it opened the gates to a Palestinian fantasy world of repatriation. Whatever else it became, UNRWA did serve to institutionalize a Palestinian position that for many years made little concession to political compromise.

"As long as UNRWA exists, it is a sign that the UN supports the Palestinian people," Hanna Siniora, editor of the Jerusalem-based Arabic daily *al-Fajr*, told me in 1984. "The camps, the schools, the clinics are the symbols." Since the intifada, Siniora would no doubt add to the list of symbols the ambulances, the RAOs, and the emergency medical facilities. New symbols and old would confirm his view that "UNRWA's work will be over when the Palestinian state is created, and not before."

I n the Six-Day War of June 1967, the Israeli army drove Egypt out of the Gaza Strip and Jordan out of the West Bank, radically transforming the situation in which Palestinian refugees had lived and UNRWA had worked for nearly 20 years.

More than 500,000 Palestinians on the West Bank crossed the Jordan River during the fighting to join about a half-million refugees already living on the East Bank. For about 175,000 of them, those whose homes were in what is now Israel, it was their second flight from the Israelis. The refugees who stayed behind on the West Bank came under the rule of Israel's military government. Reliable figures are elusive, but it is believed that just after the Six-Day War there were, in addition to the permanent Arab population, more than 300,000 refugees living in Gaza and almost as many who were living on the West Bank.

The day the fighting ended, UNRWA Commissioner-General Laurence Michelmore set out with a UN military escort from his headquarters in Beirut. Michelmore, who was living in retirement outside Washington when I interviewed him in 1983, told me he cleared the trip not only with the Israelis and UN Secretary-General U Thant, but also with the Arab governments with which UNRWA dealt. His objective, he said, was to restore as rapidly as possible under Israeli rule the services that UNRWA had rendered under the Egyptians in Gaza and the Jordanians on the West Bank.

Michelmore said that "on the spot" he made an agreement with the Israelis, ratified through an exchange of letters, that established essentially the same relations as had existed with the departed Egyptians and Jordanians. He said that from then on, as long as he remained commissioner-general, UNRWA received excellent cooperation from Israel's Foreign Ministry and had only occasional difficulties with the Israeli army.

Palestinians who remember the days of Egyptian and Jordanian rule in their country speak of it without nostalgia. Both treated the Palestinians as a subject people. If Palestinians now recall their former rulers with relative favor, it is, they admit, only because neither established colonies of settlers, as have the Israelis, who took from them their land and their water. Two decades of Israeli occupation have, nonetheless, not softened Palestinian anger toward the heavy hand of fellow Arabs who governed them from Egypt and Jordan.

The Israelis were hardly greeted as liberators when they arrived, but they were not expected to be worse, and they probably were not. In the early days, Israelis thought in terms of a "benign" occupation, a concept that has faded only slowly. Palestinian nationalism, though germinating for some decades under Arab rule, had not yet passed into an aggressive stage. Although the military administration in both the West Bank and the Gaza Strip had to contend with some *fedayeen* who identified with the PLO, popular support for them was still thin. For a decade or so, until the rightward shift in the majority in the Knesset, Israelis and Palestinians lived in sullen but generally calm coexistence.

Under Israeli occupation, material conditions in the territories changed dramatically. In 1967, the Israeli job market was opened to Arab workers, while traditional trade patterns with the Arab world were left largely undisturbed. The PLO objected to having Palestinians work in Israel but their protests went unheeded. By the time of the intifada, more than 100,000 Palestinians routinely left their homes in Gaza and the West Bank every day to work in Israel. Though the work was generally menial and the pay and benefits less than Israelis received, the occupied territories during these years were virtually without unemployment.

This meant, according to Israeli statistics, that real GNP in Gaza and the West Bank increased annually by an average of 13 percent under the occupation, while per capita income—because of the high birth rate—grew by the slightly lower figure of 11 percent. From the end of the Six-Day War until the mid-1980s, the number of cars rose tenfold and the number of licensed drivers from 6,500 to 84,000. Electricity consumption soared along with the ownership of refrigerators and television sets. Nearly nine out of ten homes had gas or electric ranges by the mid-1980s, compared to about 4 percent 20 years earlier.

In the relatively spacious West Bank, about 100,000 people, fewer than a fourth of the refugee population, now live in camps, which have themselves been much improved and now are almost indistinguishable from nearby villages. In the much more crowded Gaza Strip, some 250,000 people, more than half of the refugee population, are still jammed into camps in conditions of palpable misery. Still, according to the testimony of those who knew it before and after the Six-Day War, conditions notably improved even in Gaza.

During the same period, infant mortality declined sharply and life expectancy rose. Much of the credit belongs to UNRWA's health and sanitation services, much to Israeli efforts to improve sewerage systems, water supplies, and medical services. Even more can probably be attributed to the improvements in diet and living conditions. Whatever the explanation, the result has been as much as a doubling in the population of the territories since the war, from 950,000 to 2 million people or more. Compared to the pre-1967 era, furthermore, by the eve of the intifada these people were living in considerable prosperity.

Yet, over this period Palestinian national consciousness intensified dramatically, confounding Israel's expectations. Many Israelis had hoped, while many Palestinians feared, that prosperity would bring a decline in national passions. What experience proved, in contrast, was that Palestinian living standards bore no relation to the growth of Palestinian nationalism. The "Palestinian problem" showed itself to be relentlessly political, unyielding to even the most artful economic strategy.

After 1967, UNRWA found itself caught everywhere—in the Arab countries as well as in Israel—in the grasp of rising nationalism. The Six-Day War had left Palestinians with a disdain for the military capacities and, by extension, the social systems of the Arab nations, and roused them to contemplation of a liberation that they themselves would achieve. By the mid-1970s, the PLO had become a significant factor in their thinking, reminding them that bitter as were their feelings toward the Arabs, the enemy was still the Israelis who governed them, while tilling their land. For UNRWA, Palestinian nationalism was an element to consider in all of its sectors, but in the occupied territories it had a real potential for explosion.

At the same time, the Six-Day War produced a surge of nationalism among Israelis. Israel's yearning for peace appeared to recede before a wave of assertiveness toward Arabs in general, and toward the Palestinians in particular, making UNRWA's predicament as a nonpartisan operating agency more difficult than before.

At best, UNRWA's mission functioned within a paradox. The agency had been founded to help the Palestinians—losers in a contest that Israel had won. Although it was not expected to take sides, only in the most abstract way was it a disinterested party in the Arab-Israeli conflict. Its task was to redress, at least in some measure, the legacy of the Palestinian defeat. Almost all of its personnel was Palestinian. Its sympathies, on an official as well as a human level, were with the Palestinians. It is a wonder that it functioned at all under Israeli jurisdiction.

In official statements, the Israeli government took the position that it could do quite nicely without UNRWA. It said UNRWA did nothing that Israelis could not do better and more cheaply. UNRWA's main function, it proclaimed, was to keep an inflated payroll. Israel has long been vexed that UNRWA pays its teachers more than the Israelis pay the Palestinians who teach in government schools and pays them in Jordanian dinars, a stronger currency than the Israeli shekel. Israelis dismiss the nearly $100 million in hard currency that UNRWA spent in the occupied territories in 1988 to provide food, education, and health care, responsibilities that otherwise would have fallen on Israel's shoulders. Officially, they have taken the position that they could replace what UNRWA spends from other sources.

More damning, in Israel's eyes, is its charge that UNRWA is a barrier to history. UNRWA, Israelis argue, perpetuates the anomaly of refugee status instead of working to have its clients, like every other body of refugees in the world, integrated into the societies where they have sought refuge. The challenge of resettlement is an easy one given the cultural unity of the Arabs, the Israelis say. Israel contends that the United Nations should have cut off UNRWA's funds long ago. Admitting that such a decision would seem cruel, they have maintained that in the long run it would be humane because it would solve the refugee problem once and for all.

Yet, Israel's continued toleration of UNRWA's presence—being sovereign, it could have banished UNRWA any time it chose—sharply belies its official assertions. Israelis say UNRWA remains only because of a commitment made long ago to the UN. It concedes that the United States, as well as other governments with which Israel is friendly, would find expulsion highly objectionable. Obviously, there is more to the story. There is reason to believe, in fact, that Israel keeps UNRWA because in some ways its functions serve the nation's interest.

The conventional thinking in Israel, at least before the intifada, held that as long as the territories were politically in flux, UNRWA was a stabilizing influence, discouraging Palestinians from taking to the barricades. Some said that UNRWA's tenure in the territories would endure for only as long as it took Israel's right-wing political leadership to consolidate its rule. Ultimately, Israel would annex the West Bank and the Gaza Strip, according to this school of thought, and assume

UNRWA's functions. It is a reasonable speculation that if the government of Prime Minister Begin had achieved a political success in invading Lebanon in 1982, UNRWA's expulsion might have taken place by now. The venture in Lebanon, however, failed, and UNRWA proved itself indispensable to the Israeli army in ministering to thousands of homeless refugees. With the intifada, the political initiative has passed to the Palestinians and, though some die-hards remain, most Israelis agree that the option of annexation is no longer available. In the past year or so, talk within Israel of UNRWA's departure has consequently dropped nearly to zero.

The first decade after the Six-Day War, when the occupation was relatively quiet, UNRWA performed its duties barely noticed. Keeping a low profile, its squabbles with the government drew little attention. There were minor power struggles, remarkably similar to those UNRWA had with Syria and Jordan, over patronage hiring, protection of employees, building permits, police or military harassment. With Begin's election in 1977, however, relations began to deteriorate.

The new settlement policy established by the Begin government brought thousands of Israelis into the territories to live. Most were aggressively nationalistic, setting the stage for confrontation. By the end of the 1970s, roads that crossed Arab villages or passed the gates of refugee camps were crowded with Israeli cars. Once, Arabs had demonstrated on their national holidays and no one cared. Stones thrown by young Palestinians, once dismissed as a harmless discharge of steam, suddenly were deemed provocation. The settlers, usually armed, sometimes took the law into their own hands, but, more often, they relied on their considerable political power to summon the army and, with increasing severity, the army responded. Soldiers now toured the West Bank and the Gaza Strip with clubs, tear gas, and loaded guns. The Arabs, without arms, turned to the streets, and with each confrontation the level of violence rose a notch. During the 1980s, arrests, collective punishments, and dead or wounded teenagers became commonplace.

UNRWA contended that the Israelis were required to observe the Geneva Convention. Israel did not agree. UNRWA told the Palestinians sternly that it could not help them if they broke the law, but it stepped forth when the army arrested innocent students or slapped curfews at random on camps and villages. UNRWA particularly protested when the Israelis interfered with its own daily duties, for instance, by sealing the gates of refugee camps and thereby preventing UNRWA's trucks from carting away trash. The daily friction did not create serious antagonism, however. The Israelis respected the professionalism of UNRWA's international staff, and the staff took satisfaction in the overall effectiveness of its work. Each year, however, the lines were more sharply drawn, as UNRWA gravitated closer to the increasingly oppressed local population. Such was the condition in the West Bank and the Gaza Strip when, in December of 1987, the intifada began.

IV

UNRWA as an Institution

U NRWA employs the largest staff—more than 18,000 persons—of all the UN agencies. It has, in fact, almost as many employees as all the other UN agencies combined. It operates in five different political jurisdictions, each with its own headquarters: the West Bank and the Gaza Strip, Jordan, Syria, and Lebanon. Apart from the governments of the region, UNRWA is the largest single employer in the entire Middle East.

At the latest count, its international staff was 130, which includes two dozen on loan from the United Nations Educational, Scientific and Cultural Organization (UNESCO) for educational work and from the World Health Organization (WHO) for medical services. The internationals are UNRWA's leadership cadre, its highly skilled professionals. Almost all are Westerners, and most have entered UNRWA only after years of experience in other fields—the military, economic development, diplomacy. In cost-cutting campaigns over the past two decades, their ranks have diminished by nearly half, and management studies maintain that their number is probably too few for the ongoing administrative and technical work of the agency. But somehow the work gets done.

The Arab states have traditionally argued that more responsibility should be turned over to the Palestinians hired in the field, known in UNRWA jargon as the "area staff." But UNRWA is an agency of the United Nations, and without its professional cadre providing the leadership it would no longer be acceptable to all the players in the Arab-Israeli conflict. The area staff, although demonstrably competent, has a closer emotional involvement than the internationals in UNRWA's work. The agency's dual structure creates a natural tension, with the internationals demanding performance of a nonpolitical character, a demand to which some local employees take exception. Were the agency Palestinian, moreover, it would lose its claim to being impartial in the daily encounters in which the interests of the refugees confront those of the host governments, not just Israeli but Arab as well.

UNRWA's international headquarters, now part of the UN complex in Vienna, probably functions more impartially now than it did in Beirut. Each year the General Assembly defers to its Arab members and goes through the formality of instructing UNRWA to return to the Middle East. UNRWA does not disagree in principle. Vienna's distance from the region is unquestionably an inconvenience, but a return to Beirut is unimaginable under current conditions and, for reasons of politics and communications, no other Middle East capital seems feasible.

Beginning in 1951, UNRWA defined a refugee eligible for its aid as "a person whose normal residence was Palestine for a minimum of two years preceding the conflict in 1948 and who, as a result of this conflict, lost both his home and means of livelihood and took refuge in one of the countries where UNRWA provides relief." At that time, it also stipulated that "the direct descendants of such refugees are eligible for agency assistance." The definition has meant, on the one hand, that a small proportion of refugees—chiefly professionals, those who chose to leave the region, or persons who fled Palestine with money or personal property—were never registered as clients of UNRWA. On the other hand, it has meant that UNRWA has accepted responsibility for the offspring of registered refugees through all the generations. Since the first flight of the Palestinians, more than four decades have passed, which means that the overwhelming majority of refugees on the UNRWA rolls are too young ever to have seen their ancestral homes.

UNRWA's policy, furthermore, has been not to excise from its rolls refugees who, even by its own definition, have acquired "means of livelihood." Once registered with UNRWA, refugees stay registered, whatever their economic status. Although they may lose their eligibility for some of UNRWA's services—food rations, for example, are currently distributed only to the needy—they remain covered by whatever political promise UNRWA's existence conveys.

Over the years, the UNRWA registration card has acquired among refugees an almost sacrosanct quality. For many, it is, symbolically if not realistically, a substitute for a passport, which a large proportion of refugees are without. It is seen by most as the international community's IOU on a ticket home. For the refugee community, the UNRWA card is a documentary vow of responsibility by the United Nations for their condition, and any effort to dilute that vow is looked upon as a conspiracy.

In 1982, for example, UNRWA decided to revise its longstanding registration system in which cards covering all dependents were issued in the name of family heads. New cards, UNRWA announced, would be issued for every qualified individual. Its aims, UNRWA insisted, were in no way political but were simply to facilitate the distribution of relief services to families with members living away from home. The new cards, furthermore, would be smaller and of plastic, UNRWA said, thus more convenient than the old, weatherbeaten cards carried by the family heads.

Notwithstanding these assurances, most Palestinians saw the move, at best, as a trick for dealing with one of UNRWA's ongoing conflicts with its clientele—eliminating the dead and departed from the agency's rolls. On the protest of King Hussein's government, the new cards were never issued in Jordan or the West Bank. About half the refugees received them in Syria before a government order compelled UNRWA to stop distribution. Because of the security situation no new cards were issued in Lebanon at all, and in the Gaza Strip distribution was stopped before the task was completed. Since that time, UNRWA has returned to the original system, revalidating family registration cards in all its jurisdictions.

The resistance of the refugees to any updating of the rolls has been a longstanding nightmare to UNRWA. Arab governments have supported the tactic and have further forbidden UNRWA to conduct any census to establish precisely how many refugees there are. This obstruction probably means that the administrative rolls bear only the faintest resemblance to the actual number of refugees that UNRWA serves.

UNRWA acknowledges that its figures are inaccurate and subject to political manipulation by both Arabs and Israelis. Over the years, it has tried repeatedly to rectify its records, and they are surely less grotesque than they once were. Privately, UNRWA officials acknowledged that a "secondary benefit" of the system of individual registration that it proposed would have been a cleansing of the rolls. The failure to implement the change means that UNRWA will continue to work with approximate numbers in its planning of services to the refugee community.

In 1950, the rolls were about 1 million and, with a high refugee birth rate, they had grown to 1,350,000 by the eve of the Six-Day War in 1967. The war, by UNRWA's estimate, sent some 200,000 Palestinians—about half of them already on UNRWA's rolls—fleeing from the West Bank into Jordan. Those who were not UNRWA's clients were cared for by the Jordanian government, with the help of private charities and other UN agencies. Though no new refugees were registered as a result of the 1967 war, by

1988, UNRWA's rolls were at 2,268,000 and rising at a rate of 2 percent annually.

The relentless increase in the refugee rolls has imposed severe financial strain on UNRWA throughout its history. Some years its revenues have fallen short of needs, and deficits have been met by canceling new construction or postponing repairs. New building has taken place when possible, much of it the consequence of designated grants by individual governments or private agencies, but most of UNRWA's schools and clinics look as if they are held together by coats of paint. Quite apart from emergency programs, much of the ongoing work to which UNRWA is committed, chiefly in education, has survived by the agency's drawing on its skimpy reserves—some of it held to pay pension commitments—and cutting out other planned projects.

In the public mind, the program that most dramatically identifies UNRWA is the network of 61 refugee camps, the services for which it takes responsibility throughout the Middle East. What may not be widely realized is that of the 2,268,000 currently registered refugees less than 800,000 are camp residents. Of the five jurisdictions in which UNRWA operates, in only Gaza and Lebanon do more than half the refugees live in camps. In Syria, Jordan, and the West Bank, nearly three-fourths live, more or less normally, within cities, towns, and villages. The conventional view of the camps is that they are squalid and depressing and, indeed, some, like the swarming Rafah and Beach camps in Gaza, are barely fit for human habitation. But, over the years, the camps have all acquired some modern amenities—electricity, safe water, paved streets. In the mid-1950s, the last of the tents gave way to permanent shelters of cement-block or mud. Most shelters now have indoor latrines. Some camps are even hard to recognize. The Yarmouk camp in Damascus and the Qalandiyya camp on the West Bank, for example, have been absorbed into the cities around them. In the Jordanian countryside, the Irbid and Suf camps convey the feeling of traditional villages.

To be sure, to Western eyes, all the camps appear cramped and dirty, but the Palestinians may not perceive them in precisely that way. In general, the camps shelter not former city-dwellers accustomed to urban amenities, but poor refugees from the countryside. More than anything, the camps are a cross-section of rural Palestinian society. The refugees, in most cases, brought their social organization with them, creating living arrangements that resemble an agglomeration of villages. It is a fair observation that camp life, in many ways, is not far different from what most of the refugees left behind.

The camps are rich in Palestinian social relations, and most are convenient to jobs and marketing. Although many refugees have prospered, and some have become wealthy, few move out. Almost every camp has a waiting list of families wanting houses, if only because they are rent-free. Finances, however, are only part of the consideration. The cohesiveness of Palestinian families explains more about why the camps are not vacated. Politics aside, many families prefer to stay together in mud or cement-block houses than to be separated and live in more luxurious circumstances outside.

The camps themselves are important to the refugees' feelings that their fate has not been settled. For years, the Israelis have been trying to tear down the empty, rodent-infested mud shelters of a camp near Jericho that was all but abandoned in 1967 by refugees fleeing to Jordan. It is practically a ghost town, but the refugees who remain, suspicious of Israeli intentions, have successfully resisted the effort. The silent shelters are a bleak reminder for travelers making the overland journey between Jerusalem and Amman of the deeply rooted anguish of the Palestinian dispossessed.

One of the vivid recollections of my tour of the Gaza Strip in the early 1980s is of a heavy Palestinian woman, wearing a soiled black gown and missing a front tooth, sitting in the hot sun in front of her shelter on a dusty street in the Rafah camp. Her face bore deep lines of age and anxiety though she was probably not older than forty. Of the Gaza Strip camps, all of which are horrid, Rafah is the worst. I saw no trees to provide shade. Smelly heaps of garbage lay on the street. Children played at the edges of a fetid pool, which the authorities promised one day to drain. When I returned to the camp some years later, the fetid pool was still there.

I asked the woman whether she would like to move out of the camp to a pleasant home in a nearby town. She said no. I asked whether the camp should be rebuilt into nice neighborhoods with parks and underground sewers. She said no again. When I asked her why, she explained that she would leave her cement-block shelter, cold in winter and insufferably hot in summer, only to go back to her home, which was just a few miles away, in Israel. Until then, she would remain in Rafah, she said, her suffering a reminder to the world of the injustices done to her and her people.

Contrary to widespread belief, UNRWA does not actually operate the camps, though it takes responsibility for their overall maintenance. In all instances, UNRWA must defer to regular civil authority. A camp services officer is in charge of UNRWA services. He tries to keep the authorities, whether Arab or Israeli, out of UNRWA installations and prevent their intruding in UNRWA programs, but the camps are within sovereign jurisdiction and have no extraterritorial character. In any dispute, UNRWA holds a distinctly weaker hand.

On a day to day basis, the local police are the authority the refugees are most likely to encounter. All camps are within a local law enforcement jurisdiction and most actually have their own police posts. The local authorities patrol the streets and alleys and make their presence felt not just throughout the camp but deep inside the community. The system does not work notably better for the refugees in the Arab countries than in the occupied territories. Wherever they live, the Palestinians are a foreign element, not fully welcome, objects of suspicion in cultures where suspicion is everywhere.

It is no secret that networks of Palestinian informers report regularly to the authorities, Arab or Israeli,
serving as an integral part of a control system that blankets refugee society. The security services have no need to
engage informers by heavy-handed threats or even by
paying money. The system of inducement and coercion is
more subtle than that. What it takes is, "Muhammad, you
have such a talented daughter. We could help her to go to
the university if . . ." or "Khalid, your son got into some
trouble last night. We could keep him from going to jail
this time if . . . . " The system has succeeded everywhere
in keeping the refugees on the defensive, uncertain of one
another, cultivating their paranoia.

O ver the decades, UNRWA's impact has been most
deeply felt in its 633 elementary and preparatory
(junior high) schools which provide nine years of instruc-
tion to nearly 350,000 Palestinian children. In addition,
the agency runs eight teacher and vocational training
centers. Formerly two-year boarding schools, for economy
reasons they became day schools in 1985, except for
students classified by income or travel distance as "hardship cases." Of UNRWA's regular budget, 65 percent is
spent on the educational system. Of its 18,000-member
area staff, more than 10,000 are teachers. Based on the
results of standard tests, it can be said that UNRWA's
schools are the best in the Arab world. The enrollment of
refugee children at the elementary level is 83 percent, 73
percent at the preparatory level, notably higher than the
average for the Arab countries. Illiteracy is practically
unknown among refugee children. Agreements with the
host governments provide for secondary schooling, and
UNRWA offers university scholarships to hundreds of
graduates. It is no coincidence that well-educated Palestinians hold thousands of high posts in management and
technology not only in the Arabic-speaking countries but
throughout the world.

From its early days, UNRWA has had disputes with the host governments—and, since the occupation, particularly with Israel—over textbooks. Under the guidance of educational experts from UNESCO, UNRWA follows local school curricula, which for reasons of history mean Jordan's on the West Bank, Egypt's in Gaza. Not surprisingly, Arab textbooks contain assertions which Israelis find objectionable, but even Jordan, Lebanon, and, especially, Syria have occasionally protested UNRWA's selection of books. Tempered by a mutual commitment to the survival of the schools, the struggle to find workable compromises never ends.

UNRWA did not begin with its current sharp focus on education. After giving up in the early 1950s on its plan to create jobs in economic development projects, it decided that the next best strategy for long-term assistance was to prepare Palestinians for work in the outside world. The response of refugee parents has been overwhelming. I have often heard refugees say that, being without land, they have only education as a capital asset. UNRWA schools provide the access, but the refugees' own ambitions have become the engine of the Palestinians' academic achievement. In recent years, Palestinians have emerged as one of the world's most educated peoples. The Israeli administration is thus striking at a particularly tender spot in adopting school closings as a weapon against the intifada.

In order to put more energy and funds over the years into education, UNRWA made a deliberate decision to decrease its food relief, which had been one of its principal functions in the early days. In theory, eligibility for UNRWA's rations program had always been limited to the needy, but monitoring the ration rolls became an insuperable task and, as early as 1952, UNRWA gave up selective distribution and placed arbitrary ceilings on the food it made available to the refugees. This meant in some cases denying food to the hungry, while supplying stocks to a prospering, refugee-run black market.

Beginning in the 1970s, as oil wealth from the Gulf trickled down to reach the less fortunate Arab countries, the economic condition of the refugees steadily improved. In 1982, the commissioner-general reported that "today nearly all refugee families are self-supporting." Nonetheless, he said, 832,000 refugees, only a fraction of them in needy circumstances, were still receiving rations on a sustained basis. By now, the rations program had become a target of the donor nations, which saw it as a tremendous waste of needed resources.

It was the emergency imposed by the Israeli invasion of Lebanon, however, that persuaded UNRWA to delay no longer what had long seemed inevitable. The unprecedented burden that accompanied the invasion made a shift in priorities essential. To facilitate the changeover, UNRWA negotiated with the European Community an agreement to shift to an annual cash payment the $15 million in foodstuffs it had been contributing to the agency. With these funds available as a backstop, UNRWA in September 1982 formally announced the end of its basic rations program.

Since then, the agency has limited its rations distributions to school lunches for children and high-protein food supplements for infants. In addition, it has distributed food to verified "hardship cases"—families without males of working age, which in practice chiefly mean widows and the aged. The savings of $32.4 million in the first year permitted a diversion of funds, after the costs of Lebanese relief, to UNRWA's schools. At last count, UNRWA had 32,000 families representing 135,000 refugees—16 percent of the number it had in 1982—registered on its "hardship" rolls.

Accompanying the change, however, was the problem of verification of "hardship," which the refugees saw as policing. At the same time, the Arab countries worried that the decision was a first step in UNRWA's abdication of its responsibilities. Though there was little dispute with UNRWA's placing of education above rations on its list of priorities, the Arab world reacted with apprehension and the agency's popularity declined.

Syria, arguing that all refugees were by nature hardship cases, refused authorization to UNRWA to conduct the verification proceedings. Resorting to strategems, the UNRWA office in Damascus initiated the hardship program anyway. Finally, after a visit by the commissioner-general and a series of warnings, the Syrian government quietly acquiesced in the new policy.

In the General Assembly session in the fall of 1983, Jordan introduced a resolution denouncing "the interruption by the Agency of the general ration distribution to the Palestinian refugees . . . " and demanded its prompt resumption. The resolution passed by 123 to 19, but under UN rules it was not enforceable over UNRWA's objections. Only the major donor countries endorsed the change, voting in the negative.

Each fall, the UN's Special Political Committee reviews UNRWA's activities of the previous year and votes on resolutions that bear on UNRWA's future. Traditionally, this review has been a forum for a wide-ranging debate on Middle East issues in which Arab and Israeli delegates swing freely at each other. In the course of the debate of 1982, for example, Jordanian Ambassador Abdullah Salah charged UNRWA with acting as if "the only solution to the financial crisis in the agency was to continue to reduce basic services." Significantly, he claimed no *economic* need for the rations program. Privately, in fact, he made known his approval of UNRWA's decision to give the schools a higher priority than the food, but, he said, "Jordan wished . . . to caution against the tendency to reduce services, which would mean, in the final analysis, the beginning of the liquidation of the Agency."

Salah went further, blaming Israel for conspiring to end UNRWA in order to erase the refugees from the UN agenda. All of UNRWA's programs must remain intact, he declared, "because the Agency and the services it provide(s) reflect the international community's recognition

of the rights and the tragedy of the Palestinian people
. . . ." As do other Arab delegates, Jordan's still argues
routinely at the UN for restoration of the basic rations
program as a reaffirmation of Palestinian rights.

For years, Israel criticized the Arab states severely
for failing to make larger contributions to UNRWA's
budgets, to which the Arabs replied that they already carry
a far heavier burden than the major donor nations simply
by caring for the refugee communities within their borders. In recent years, the Arabs have increased their
contributions and the issue has become less sensitive.
Arab gifts to UNRWA's emergency fund for the intifada
have, in fact, been generous. Nonetheless, as a matter of
principle, Arab delegates have continued to argue that,
being the victims, not the makers, of the refugee problem,
they have no obligation to UNRWA. They also repeat
their suspicions that once their gifts are taken for granted,
the West will abdicate its own responsibility for the
condition of the refugees, leaving the Arab world to
assume the bulk of UNRWA's expenses alone.

"The Israelis are trying to turn UNRWA into a
humanitarian issue," a Jordanian spokesman at the UN
said to me. "But we're not buying that. The refugee issue
is not and will never be simply a humanitarian question. It
has and will remain a political question, and will be
resolved by political means."

Recently, observers have noted that the pitch of the
annual debate in the Special Political Committee has
toned down a trifle and that UNRWA has become less of
a pawn in the exchange of propaganda charges. It remains
conventional for the Israeli delegate to chide the Arabs for
refusing to solve the problems of the refugees on their
own, and for the Arabs to reply by denouncing Israel for
refusing to implement the instructions of the General
Assembly to permit the refugees' repatriation. The language, however, has become more muted. Meanwhile,
both Arabs and Israelis continue to vote their endorsement of UNRWA's programs and in favor of UNRWA's
annual budget.

U NRWA's most acute financial problems came in the early 1980s, which was the most highly ideological period of the Reagan administration in Washington. UNRWA became one of its targets.

The United States had for some years been making a contribution to UNRWA that was roughly a third of its budget. In contrast, the Soviet bloc, arguing that UNRWA was born of Western imperialism in the Middle East, gave nothing. The Arabs at that time were still contributing only a pittance. Besides the United States, UNRWA's major donors were the European countries and Japan, along with the European Community as a bloc. All let themselves be guided by the size of Washington's contribution, creating among the administrators of UNRWA the apprehension that even a modest American cutback would signal a general retreat.

Within the Reagan administration, some thinkers objected to UNRWA because it was a relief organization, violating their conservative ideology. Others regarded it as anti-Israel and pro-PLO, and thus an obstacle to America's security objectives in the region. Some maintained that UNRWA, in not being managed rigorously enough, was wasteful of American taxpayers' dollars.

In contrast to the Reagan ideologues, the professional diplomats in the administration strongly supported UNRWA. They argued that by enhancing regional stability, it served not only American but Israeli interests. They also contended that, within the context of a policy generally perceived as pro-Israeli, Washington's central role in supporting UNRWA kept the doors open to the leaders of the Arab states.

Washington's attitude remained a cloud over UNRWA's operations through the summer of 1982, when Israel invaded Lebanon, changing the configuration of power in the Middle East. The invasion imposed on UNRWA, beyond its normal budgetary burdens, the costs of a huge program of emergency relief. At the very moment that UNRWA leaders were laboring to devise a plan to meet these expenses, an emissary from Washington arrived in Vienna with the message that the United States intended to cut its contribution from $67 million to $50 million in 1983. More important, he said Washington planned to phase out further contributions to zero by 1986. A shocked staff at the headquarters wondered whether they had received the announcement of UNRWA's demise.

The messenger, however, had overstated the case. In the light of Israel's experience in Lebanon, Washington, in fact, had decided to reexamine its position on UNRWA. With autumn settling over Lebanon and cold weather only weeks away, the Israelis foresaw crisis unless they found shelter for thousands of homeless refugees. Only UNRWA could meet that crisis, leaving the anti-UNRWA forces in the Reagan administration in the untenable posture of being more anti-Palestinian than the Israelis.

Then, on September 1, President Reagan announced a new peace initiative from which it was possible to conclude that the United States would not risk its relations with the Arab leadership over the UNRWA donation. In early 1983, Washington announced it would contribute not only the full $67 million expected of it but also an additional $17 million toward Lebanese relief. Two years later, with UNRWA once again in budgetary trouble, the Reagan administration came to the agency's assistance with a timely gift of $8 million, which the European Community equaled.

If the return of the United States to the donors' fold helped solve the crises of the early 1980s, its contributions were by no means enough to put UNRWA on a permanently sound footing. Each year, UNRWA requires an increase of about 5 percent—taking into account natural population growth and inflation—simply to maintain basic programs at an unchanged level. The shoestring nature of the financing process is apparent in the 1988 budget of just $224 million, less than the 1985 budget of $232 million. At $234 million, the 1989 budget is just a shade higher.

UNRWA's traditional donors, their generosity strained by the demands imposed by Lebanon and the intifada, have not kept pace with the increases in expenditures. In 1988 the United States, under budgetary constraints at home, once again cut its contribution, though the European Community and its members, after a dip in the mid-1980s, have recently given more generously. Apart from the Arab gifts of recent years, UNRWA has had little success in widening the circle of reliable donors.

"It is probably endemic with organizations that depend on voluntary contributions always to be in water up to the nostrils," said Commissioner-General Giacomelli in our talk. "We never seem able to get our head fully out of the water.

"The Arabs say 'Don't budget according to what you get but according to what you need,' but that's day-dreaming. We have instituted a range of austerity measures, and we have adopted procedures to bring the donor countries into the planning process so that our income is now reasonably in line with what we propose. We thought we had reached some equilibrium point, and then in '86 the camp war started in Lebanon and in '87 the uprising in the West Bank and Gaza. We can't make special appeals year after year. The donors get tired of hearing it. The intifada forced them to have another look at what was happening in the Middle East, but the crises go on and on.

"However the situation ultimately stabilizes, it will probably require a higher level than before of activity in the field, and right now we're running out of money again. Pretty soon the two curves of increased voluntary donations and expenditures will cross. We have enough to last through 1989 but by next year we'll have to go back with more appeals. And what will we tell them then?"

Giacomelli, who seems by nature not to be much given to emotional statements, is also aware of the limitations on political posturing imposed by the administrative character of his position. Yet, in his most recent report to the General Assembly, he could not resist volunteering a warning that UNRWA may have reached the limit of what it can do and that the grim situation is unlikely to be relieved except by a serious effort at making peace.

"What is the answer," he wrote, "to this basic divergence between mounting demands for agency services and the prospect of, at best, a stable level of income? The most obvious answer is, of course, that we hope to be relieved of this dilemma through the commencement of a viable Middle East peace process that would point the way for UNRWA to begin making plans for gradually relinquishing the responsibilities given to it by the international community. . . . It is not, of course, up to the commissioner-general of UNRWA to suggest what form a settlement should take or how best to achieve it. But I would be remiss in my duty if I did not urge in the strongest possible way that the peace process, whatever form it may take, start at the earliest possible moment. In the meantime, to the extent that our resources allow, we will continue to do our best."

V

UNRWA in Lebanon

U NRWA's most serious challenge between the Six-
Day War in 1967 and the intifada 20 years later came
with the Israeli invasion of Lebanon in June 1982. The
threat to the lives of the Palestinians who had taken refuge
in that country imposed an unprecedented burden on
UNRWA's resources and upon its resourcefulness. To
keep the refugees fed and sheltered, UNRWA, in an
emergency appeal, raised $50 million above its regular
budget. Its staff reacted to the challenge of danger and
difficulty with a level of courage and ingenuity that belies
the bad reputation that bureaucracy has acquired in our
time.

South Lebanon was the principal battlefield in the
war. In launching the invasion, the Israelis' objective was
to destroy the PLO forces which, through raids and shelling from bases there, had cast a shadow over daily life in
northern Israel. Nearly 200,000 Palestinians lived in south
Lebanon, most of them refugees from the flight in 1948
from Haifa and the Galilee. The majority had their homes
in the refugee camps where the PLO's strength was concentrated. At the time of the invasion, the Israelis com-
municated to the refugees a warning to leave the camps.

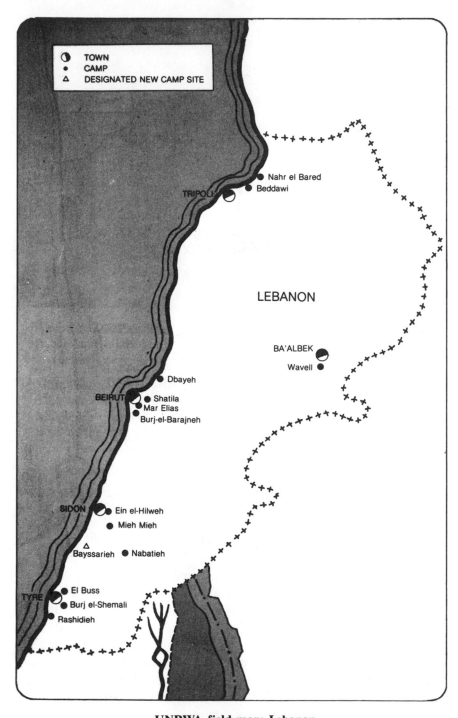

UNRWA field map: Lebanon
Registered refugee population in Lebanon: 288,176
Proportion of total registered refugee population: 13%

They then dropped bombs and shells. The destruction heaped on the camps left UNRWA with little choice. The debilitated Lebanese government made clear, early on, that it would look after only Lebanese victims of the war, not Palestinians. If UNRWA did not take responsibility for the refugees, no one would. In the initial days, UNRWA's Beirut office geared up to bring in supplies to beleaguered Palestinians, whether or not they were registered refugees, as soon as there was a lull in the fighting.

On June 20, two weeks after the Israeli forces crossed the frontier, the first convoy set out from Beirut to the south. In the lead car, flying a UN flag, were members of UNRWA's international staff whose mission was to deal with the political problems of the rescue mission. Local employees drove the trucks. En route, the convoy had to pass successively the checkpoints of the PLO, the Syrians, the Muslim Murabitun, the Christian Lebanese Forces, and, lastly, the Israelis. The Israeli army had officially approved the mission but at all the checkpoints, the staff had to argue its case. Finally, the convoy reached its destination, bringing food to the hungry, blankets to the homeless. By the end of the month, five such convoys had reached the south.

The Israeli siege of Beirut, which in mid-summer cut off the UNRWA regional office from its clients, required the organization of new lines of logistical support. Further complications were imposed on the relief operations by the flight to the north and east of thousands of refugees seeking quieter sections of the country. Some even sought out Syria as a haven. With the cooperation of the Israeli and Syrian authorities, UNRWA initiated relief shipments to south Lebanon from Jerusalem and to east and north Lebanon from Damascus. In Syria, the refugees were placed under the care of UNRWA's Damascus headquarters. These improvised arrangements lasted more than a year.

It was not because food was short on the local market in Lebanon that rations were needed. The problem was the massive loss of income among Palestinian families whose men had gone off to fight or been interned by the Israelis. Recognizing that the situation would not quickly improve, UNRWA recommitted itself to the general distribution of rations in Lebanon, although this program was being phased out elsewhere. A commitment was made to maintain the program at least until the spring of 1984.

I watched an UNRWA officer in south Lebanon distribute these rations from the tailgate of a truck one day in 1983. Several dozen Palestinian women, many of them tattooed, some carrying babies, all wearing long, colorful, but soiled dresses, crowded around screaming aggressively, without embarrassment demanding more. Six years later, on the morning that UNRWA was unsuccessful in distributing food at the Shufat camp, I was reminded of this scene. I recalled asking the UNRWA man in charge, himself a Palestinian, whether the women were humiliated at having to struggle for this charity. On the contrary, he said, the food is a status symbol showing that the woman knows how to work the system. It also shows that her family is the object of the UN's concern.

UNRWA in those months distributed not only food but such items as soap and towels, mattresses and clothing, and kitchen equipment and cooking stoves. To avert epidemics, UNRWA health teams labored to provide sanitation services and supplies of potable water in the badly disorganized camps.

Perhaps UNRWA's finest achievement was to resume the operation of its schools. The children were widely scattered. The teaching staff, much of which had also vanished in the fighting, had to be reassembled. Yet, despite the chaotic conditions, half the schools were reopened by October and most of the rest by December 1982. Some were put on triple shifts and several were set up in tents. By early 1983, nearly 33,000 children were in class, only slightly fewer than the year before.

UNRWA also took responsibility for rebuilding refugee housing in the combat area, more than 50 percent of which had been destroyed. Its initial plan to establish new, temporary camps was vetoed by the Lebanese government, which was convinced that once built, they would never be dismantled. The Israelis, who would have preferred that there be no camps at all, also refused permission for new installations. So UNRWA began clearing the rubble within the old camp boundaries. New plots were assigned, although much of the effort was frustrated by gross land-grabbing by some of the refugees.

For UNRWA, dealing with the refugees was hardly easier than dealing with the military authorities. Chronically angry, the refugees were less than ever in a cooperative frame of mind. Since their flight into Lebanon in 1948, they had painstakingly rebuilt the routine of their lives, however unsatisfactory, in the face of huge obstacles. Since the arrival of PLO military units in the early 1970s, the Israelis had routinely attacked their camps with artillery and aircraft, even with naval guns, making life miserable. In early 1978, the Israeli army had occupied the south of Lebanon for three months, destroying Palestinian installations in a vain effort to deny a haven to PLO guerrilla forces. In 1982, the Israeli invasion had beaten the Palestinians again. When UNRWA brought them tents as temporary shelter, it brought back bleak memories of the early days on the run, and many burned the tents in protest.

That fall, with cold weather coming on, UNRWA adopted the policy of providing cash grants to permit refugees to construct their own homes. With the help of construction materials supplied by international volunteer agencies, the program moved ahead. Throughout the winter the refugees survived in largely improvised facilities but, by spring, most of the housing in the camps had been rebuilt.

I had first toured the refugee camps in south Lebanon two years before, in the summer of 1981. I was surprised then how habitable they appeared, save for the sectors damaged in the periodic bombing and shelling of the Israelis. Whatever their bitterness inside, people even seemed rather cheerful to me. I passed briefly through the region a year later, just after the invasion, while the Israelis were still in charge, and these same camps were in shambles. By the fall of 1983, when I visited for a third time, most of the refugees who fled from the south had drifted back, and the camps were once more full of life. Few young men were around, but children and old people were busy with cement blocks and mortar. The schools were functioning, and the camps did not seem appreciably different from when I first saw them two years earlier.

But if life was once again "normal," it was a kind of normality that was unique to Lebanon. Since the start of the civil war in 1975, Lebanon was, as one UNRWA official put it in a significantly understated metaphor, a "fruit salad" of parties and factions. All of them exercised quasi-sovereign powers over some "turf." UNRWA had to enter these factors into almost every calculation.

For more than a decade prior to the invasion, the faction that most preoccupied UNRWA was the PLO. Under an agreement signed with Lebanon's divided and nearly powerless government in 1969, the PLO ran the refugee camps. In practice, it also governed south Lebanon. Because the PLO played the role of sovereign in the area of UNRWA's work, the agency had no option but to accommodate it.

UNRWA's principal differences with the PLO had been over patronage, a routine problem in the region. UNRWA's objective was to hire people qualified and willing to work in the agency's interest. It ran head-on into the PLO, intent on establishing control over UNRWA jobs, which not only paid rather well but, in many cases, provided access to useful information. Every UNRWA field office had long taken for granted that it was riddled with informers. The agency's response was to acknowledge that it probably could not eliminate dual loyalties, but it would fight to keep patronage from impairing its effectiveness. In fact, UNRWA's patronage disputes in Lebanon with the PLO were no more severe than those it experienced in every other country where it worked.

Otherwise, UNRWA's relations with the PLO were very good. The PLO protected UNRWA installations. It worked with UNRWA to make improvements in the camps. Its medical facilities complemented UNRWA's clinics. It cooperated in UNRWA's educational programs and provided university scholarships to the graduates of UNRWA schools. The PLO even gave donations to UNRWA, but after the Israeli invasion, the agency was profoundly embarrassed upon learning that the PLO had betrayed it in an UNRWA vocational training center in Siblin, a town in south Lebanon.

"The PLO put in military instructors to run afternoon courses," said John Defrates, who was then UNRWA's director in Beirut. "The principal of the school, an UNRWA employee, collaborated in this, and even made military training a requirement for a diploma. He was working for the PLO as much as for UNRWA. He used much skill to conceal from us what was happening. The trainees didn't want it. They didn't want to fight. They took off like rabbits when the Israeli army came. But for UNRWA, it created a very serious crisis."

The Siblin incident broke at the very moment that the ideologues in the Reagan administration were mounting their attack on UNRWA. For several years, every payment from Washington to UNRWA had been routinely covered by a letter warning that the money could not be used "to furnish assistance to any refugee who is receiving military training as a member of the so-called Palestine Liberation Army or any other guerrilla-type organization, or who has engaged in any act of terrorism." UNRWA's nemeses in Washington argued that the agency's staff should have known of the PLO's activity at Siblin, if in fact it did not. They also insisted that the episode was a foreseeable consequence of UNRWA's intimate relationship with the PLO, as well as of its mandate to provide aid to the Palestinians.

UNRWA accepted responsibility for negligence at Siblin and expressed its chagrin at the PLO's deception. Though UNRWA did not discipline any supervisory personnel, it dismissed the principal and most of the senior staff of the training center. Though publicly remorseful, UNRWA officials complained privately that the Israelis had exploited the incident for propaganda against the agency, and that the Americans had overreacted.

By the time the fighting in Lebanon ended, UNRWA's operational geography had changed again. The Israelis, not the PLO, occupied the heavily Palestinian areas in the south and the Lebanese army, effectively under the command of the Maronite leader Bashir Gemayel, controlled the Beirut region where the refugee camps of Sabra, Shatila, and Burj al-Barajnah were located. The PLO's military forces had retreated to two refugee camps in the north near Tripoli, and both of them soon came under the siege of Palestinian rebels linked to Syria.

"Our first thought had been to abolish the camps entirely and disperse the refugees," said Shamay Cahana, who was then director of UN affairs for the Israeli foreign ministry. "But where? Our own experts wanted to push them farther and farther north, but most of that was Maronite territory, and the Maronites wanted them out of Lebanon altogether. No one talked of admitting them to Israel.

"Meanwhile, the refugees were living wherever they could find places, and the Lebanese were being inhuman to them. When the refugees started drifting back to where they had been, to the camps in the south, the Lebanese had to let them rebuild, and by then our position was passive. We had given up our grand political ambitions for Lebanon and had become more or less reconciled to the *status quo ante* for the refugees. We wanted to turn the whole problem over to the international community, and nobody but UNRWA would take it."

In the fall of 1982, UNRWA's relationship with Israel's occupation army in Lebanon was, at best, correct. Heavily criticized for the invasion at home as well as abroad, the Israeli government did not want to estrange public opinion any further than it had by imposing more hardship on the refugees. For a time, the Israeli army had allowed hostile Lebanese militias to terrorize the refugees; Israelis had stood by passively during the massacres at Sabra and Shatila, but by the spring of 1983, the Israeli army had put a stop to Lebanese abuses, though the surveillance of its own contingents had lightened only marginally. By now, however, Israel had recognized that UNRWA could be useful and dropped its propaganda campaign over Siblin. In the field, the army adopted a policy of cooperating with UNRWA—though not without some ongoing tension—in the delivery to the refugees of food and services and in the provision of shelter.

Meanwhile, in the north, far from the Israeli lines, UNRWA faced an entirely separate war—between Palestinian factions. In the UN tradition, the agency showed no preferences among the diverse ingredients of the Lebanese "fruit salad." As long as the faction loyal to PLO Chairman Arafat remained in charge of the camps, UNRWA deferred to it in its daily operations. When Arafat's people were superseded by the rival faction of Abu Musa, favored by the Syrians, the agency shifted its dealings to reflect the new *de facto* authority.

For a time in the fall of 1983, the UNRWA staff was subject to fire almost every day in the northern region. At one point, the field office in Tripoli was hit by shells and had to move to other quarters. UNRWA's relief trucks on their way to the camps were forced to pass under the guns of not only the Christians, Syrians, and Palestinians, but also of an Islamist faction that had taken over from a communist faction in Tripoli.

UNRWA's most serious problems at that time arose in the Beirut area. In south Lebanon, Israel's quarrel was not so much with the refugees as with the PLO, while in the north PLO factions were interested only in quarreling with each other. In contrast, the narrow region around Beirut came under the control of the Christian-dominated Lebanese government, which blamed the Palestinians for the country's woes and resolved to use the powers it had acquired with Israel's assistance to make life for the refugees as insecure as possible. While the Israelis were nearby, a multinational force of French, Italian, and British troops provided some protection, patrolling the camps. In the period right after the 1984 Israeli withdrawal, the physical and economic abuses inflicted on the refugees by Lebanese bureaucrats and armed men, though not as bloody as the infamous Sabra and Shatila massacres, were still quite awful.

An incident I witnessed in the Shatila camp in October 1983, remains vividly with me, an example of the kind of problem UNRWA encountered in dealing with refugees who had so long been battered from every side. At the time, a squad of French troops, concerned about the prospect of an attack by a Shi'i faction, was stationed on the roof of an UNRWA school where they had set up an observation post. For some weeks, UNRWA had pleaded with the French commander to remove them on the grounds that their presence made the school a military target, jeopardizing the lives of hundreds of children. Having appealed in vain all the way to Paris, UNRWA took what it considered the only prudent course: it closed the school.

The Palestinians reacted with a paranoia that could only have been the product of too many years of colonialism and exile. It was a reaction shaped by the Palestinians' cultural disposition to see conspiracy everywhere and by their peculiar conviction that their best weapon against a hostile world was their own suffering.

I sat in the shabby office of the camp services officer in Shatila while the UNRWA representative, an Englishman, met with six middle-aged mukhtars who spoke for the refugees. The mukhtars said they would not be fooled, knowing that the *real* reason the school was closed had nothing to do with the children's safety. It was all a link in a British-American plot, they said, to drive France out of the Middle East, and as Palestinians they would not be victimized by these Big Power squabbles. Neither the UNRWA representative nor I could believe what we were hearing.

If UNRWA persisted in keeping the school closed, they went on, the inhabitants of the camp would retaliate by withdrawing all of their children from the educational system for the remainder of the year. Though the children would get no learning, they said, UNRWA would suffer the embarrassment of seeing its schools in the camp fall into disuse. The argument continued for several hours, and a deadlock was finally averted only by a promise made by the UNRWA man to try once more to persuade the French to leave. I subsequently learned, several weeks later, that the French did leave.

Afterward, the Palestinians stayed on to talk to me. "Visitors who come here look at us as if we were in a museum," one mukhtar said. "Then they go home and forget." He was probably right about that. The UN, having provoked their flight to Lebanon in 1948 by voting to create Israel, is to blame for their condition, the mukhtars agreed. They added, however, that without UNRWA, they might not survive. "Only UNRWA," the senior mukhtar said to me, "does not forget."

When the multinational force departed in the wake of the Israelis, the Syrians moved to regain the control of the Beirut region that they had lost in the first weeks of the invasion. No less hostile than the Israelis, the Syrians were determined to root out vestiges of PLO power in the camps and impose their will upon the Palestinian residents. To this end, they first used Amal, the Shi'i militia, and later the dissident Palestinians under Abu Musa. They kept the camps under siege, raining down shells on the inhabitants, with rare periods of respite, until 1988 when the last holdouts surrendered. Shortly afterward, an UNRWA survey revealed that 85 percent of all dwellings had been destroyed in Shatila and 60 percent in Burj al-Barajnah. Throughout most of this period, only UNRWA made a serious effort to keep the refugees alive.

Notwithstanding the intensity of the fighting, UNRWA kept its schools open most of the time. It improvised, insofar as possible, shelters for the homeless, and delivered basic health services to the inhabitants, at least to the point of averting major epidemics. It also succeeded in keeping hunger at bay by distributing, under the most hazardous conditions, emergency rations both to refugees and non-refugees in the besieged areas.

"Our problem was never food," said Franke de Jonge, the current UNRWA director in Lebanon. "Our warehouses were full in both east and west Beirut. Some of our supplies came from Damascus but much arrived at the port of Beirut, which was a difficult place because different militias exercised control, and we often had to use bribes to move across checkpoints just to get out of the port area. The real problem was the security of our delivery system to the camps. UNRWA has calculated that security, in all its forms, costs the agency an extra $1.7 million a year in Lebanon. That includes five staff members assigned only security duties, bullet-proof cars, radio equipment, escort costs, extra office and warehouse space, and lost time. Everything is doubled up because of our security needs."

I first encountered de Jonge, now 50 years old, when I was touring UNRWA installations in 1983. He is a tall, lanky Dutchman who has a wife and four children back home. Ordained as a minister in the Dutch Reformed Church, he has been working with refugees in the Middle East since 1971 and has been with UNRWA since 1979. De Jonge was UNRWA's deputy director in Lebanon at the time of our first meeting, but the director was out of the country at the time and he was in charge.

In retrospect those days seem almost peaceful, in a Lebanon that has since become even more chaotic. The airport was open when I arrived, and I was scheduled to fly out a few days hence, but the Christians and Druze began shelling each other. When the airport was ordered closed, I assumed it would open in a day or so, but de Jonge understood that conditions were deteriorating very quickly, and he decided to get me out of town while he could. I resented his invitation to depart, but UNRWA had agreed to my visit on the condition that it provide for my safety, and he allowed me no other option. De Jonge commandeered an UNRWA car, in which I was driven through the Israeli army lines to Lebanon's southern border, and I crossed into Israel on foot.

Five years later, I ran into de Jonge again on the ferry from Cyprus to the port of Juniyah, just north of Beirut; the airport was still closed and there was no viable overland route into Beirut which was my destination. A few days later, we met for breakfast in an east Beirut restaurant where I remember his insisting, for security reasons, that we take a table as far as possible from the windows. I asked him at the time whether the armored car in which he arrived really made a difference to his safety. He said it is estimated that there are more than 600 such cars in Lebanon, and they have on many occasions saved the lives of their passengers, most notably from car bombs. He also said it saved passengers—including himself, one time—from kidnapping.

De Jonge explained that, conventionally, kidnappers in Lebanon start by blocking the road with their own car, then smash the front and side windows of the target car with their rifle butts and pull out the occupants. This procedure fails in an armored car, he said, because the glass will not break. The driver is equipped with a loud speaker, he said, which announces to the kidnappers that the car cannot be penetrated. It also tells them that the occupants have radioed for help, which is on the way. At that point, he said, his own experience demonstrated that the abductors, seeing that their intended victim has the advantage, move on to some other prey.

In my research on UNRWA in 1983, I had myself experienced a second-hand encounter with the kidnapping phenomenon. On arriving for a visit at the UNRWA clinic in a refugee camp near Tyre in south Lebanon, I found a half-dozen staff members standing around in obvious shock. A jeep carrying two armed men had come by a half-hour earlier, they explained, and abducted their door-keeper. The UNRWA official who was escorting me immediately radioed the information to his headquarters, but the chances of finding the man seemed slight because no one knew who had taken him or why.

Kidnapping—or hostage-taking, if it had a political objective—became a commonplace art, applied not just to Lebanese but to Westerners. At least part of the explanation for this new phenomenon lies in the arrival in Lebanon—thanks to the hospitality of the Syrians—of a contingent of 2,000 to 3,000 armed men from revolutionary Iran. These Iranians organized a radical Shi'i militia called Hizballah, committed to the establishment of an Islamic republic and faithful to the late Ayatollah Ruhollah Khomeini. Some Lebanese kidnapping teams exist only to collect ransom, but almost all of the *political* abductions in the ensuing years are believed to be the responsibility of Hizballah operating on the orders of Tehran. As of this writing, nine Americans, several of them journalists, were hostages in Lebanon, some for years.

UNRWA has not remained immune from this scourge. Its international staff members, in fact, use black humor in referring to themselves as "the biggest body of kidnap fodder left in Lebanon." Some of the Western embassies have larger staffs, but its members are not out in the streets as part of their daily work, as is most of UNRWA's international staff.

In 1985, Alec Collett, a British journalist, was kidnapped while working temporarily for UNRWA; he is widely presumed to be dead. In February 1988, two internationals, Jan Stening of Sweden and William Jorgensen of Norway, were taken hostage—the abduction, apparently nonpolitical, was not blamed on Hizballah—but were freed three weeks later. UNRWA insists it paid no ransom and gave no other concessions for them, though sources familiar with the incident add portentously that the disclaimer does not necessarily apply to the Swedish or Norwegian governments. In addition to the international victims, 33 members of UNRWA's local staff in Lebanon were killed between 1982 and 1988, many of them while on official duty, and at least 8 more remain listed as missing.

My conversation in the spring of 1989 with Franke de Jonge did not take place in Beirut but in Damascus, where he had traveled to meet me. Over the course of the previous year, Lebanon had become so much more dangerous, particularly to Western journalists, that this time UNRWA would not take responsibility for my safety. It became so dangerous, in fact, that in April 1988 shortly after I left the region, UNRWA transferred its field office to the training center in Siblin, near Tyre, leaving only a few guards behind to watch over the property in Beirut. By prearrangement, de Jonge drove in an armored car to Damascus, which is about an hour away by road. I was grateful for his courtesy; he was glad to get out of the city for a day.

The constant strain on the 2,400 members of the UNRWA staff in Lebanon—of which 12 are internationals—is devastating, de Jonge told me. Most work six, sometimes seven, days a week, often from early morning to late at night. To provide a break in the routine, the agency has established a training program at a resort hotel in Cyprus, and senior staff members are rotated there at regular intervals for courses in management, personnel, computers, or special education. UNRWA also tries to rotate staff members to posts in the north, where a change in scenery provides some relief from daily tension. Unlike the local staff, the internationals do not have their families nearby, and so are authorized four or five trips a year to Vienna where they can combine two days of duty with some days of annual leave for reunions with wives and children. All of the internationals are limited to 18 months of service in Lebanon.

"To deliver the food," de Jonge said, continuing our discussion on security practices in Lebanon, "we have to be particularly careful in choosing our drivers. As a general rule, the UN flag we fly is honored at all the checkpoints, but you can never be certain. We assign two full-time security officers to collect and analyze the available information for questions like this: Who is likely to present what sort of obstacles at the various checkpoints? And, of course, all our vehicles carry armed security guards.

"As drivers, we've hired Sunnis and Christians and Shi'ites loyal to Amal—the moderate rivals of Hizballah—for our staff, and we pick them for each assignment according to their route and their destination. Each is a kind of ethnic specialist. We wouldn't want to have a Christian driver going through a Syrian checkpoint. We put a lot of effort every day into deciding which roads are safe. If our trucks are going south, we might take the coast road or we might go up over the mountains. We rarely are tempted to take the shortest route, even into and out of the city.

"Our intelligence also consists of establishing who holds the power at any given moment in each of the refugee camps. We have to keep in touch with the different factions all the time. That's a big part of our job.

"Arafat's Fatah people are in control in the south. The Beirut camps are mostly under the PLO factions beholden to Syria, which has the firepower, though these camps have elements inside that are loyal to the factions of George Habash and Nayif Hawatmeh. The Ayn al-Hilwah camp—which has 60,000 residents, the largest in the Middle East—though basically Fatah, has all of the PLO factions represented, including Abu Nidal. We even have a few old Nasirites there. The camps in the north are under the control of the Syrians through Abu Musa. But we also recognize that 90 percent of the refugees there, though they may render homage to [Hafiz al-] Asad and the Syrians, are pro-Arafat. Finally, we have 22,000 refugees in east Beirut, most of them Christian Palestinians, and they depend on the Christian forces.

"UNRWA has three armored cars in Lebanon, and those with armor are not distinguishable from those without. Our senior officials are required to use them, covered by a team of bodyguards. We also have different teams of bodyguards, Christian for the Christian areas, Sunnis or Shi'ites for the Muslim areas. To go from my office to the camps in the south of Lebanon, I routinely have to change bodyguards three times, as a I travel from one militia's turf to the next.

"You wouldn't believe it, but in all of this madness the politicians still retain their sensitivities about protocol. For example, if I call on General [Michel] Aoun, the Christian head, in the morning, it immediately becomes known. It's often on television. So I've got to call on Prime Minister [Salim al-] Hoss, the Muslim head, in the afternoon. If I see the Maronite patriarch one day, I've got to see the Sunni mufti the next. Even with Lebanon in disintegration, UNRWA has to maintain the niceties of diplomacy.

"The security officer keeps long lists on Lebanon's personalities, a catalogue of who belongs to whom. Everyone has a label and a contact. I'm not talking just about militias but about contractors, businessmen, officials. Lebanon, after all, made its reputation as a commercial society, and that quality has not totally disappeared.

"Usually our local employees understand the subtleties of the system of preferences better than the internationals. We are always in fights with the authorities in control over construction contracts and patronage positions, and the locals help us a lot. Sometimes it takes all our diplomatic skills and months of negotiations to settle these disputes. Everyone in Lebanon has a tie to somebody else, and these connections are something we simply cannot ignore. Knowing how to work the system can make the difference in survival. Somehow the system holds together, but we seem very often to be hanging by our fingertips.

"It's a big help that UNRWA has the reputation that anyone can approach us; we're never accused of having our own favorites in these contract and patronage disputes, of being anyone's permanent operative. When we were trying to get supplies into the camps during the most recent shelling, we had to make a little payoff to Amal in the form of food, but we were never charged with giving special favors to them or any other faction, even the Palestinians. Everyone knows we have a job to do, but we were seen as a stabilizing force, one of the very few that remain here.

"I think our image is quite different in Lebanon from what it is in the West Bank and the Gaza Strip. Because of the adversarial structure—Israel versus the Palestinians—UNRWA is seen as lined up with one of the two sides. But the Lebanese respond to us as representatives of the international community. They feel very deeply the constant threat of abandonment by the outside world. With the embassies closing down, with international businesses long since gone and very few social service agencies still here, Christians, Muslims, and Druze alike see us as just about the last visible sign that the world cares about what is going on in Lebanon.

"When our two Scandinavians [Stening and Jorgensen] were kidnapped last year, UNRWA finally let it be known that we might have to leave, too. We said we simply could no longer put up with such abuses. A bit to our surprise, the entire country, all the factions, rallied to our support. It certainly was not because we are identified with the Palestinians. On the contrary, most Lebanese don't give a damn about the Palestinians. It was because we are a channel of communication to the United Nations secretary-general and to the General Assembly. It was also that we stand for some faint hope that the outside world will at some point come in and restore sanity among the Lebanese."

Before de Jonge left Damascus to return to Beirut, I asked him whatever happened to the training center at Siblin that had caused the crisis for UNRWA in 1982. He told me it had been a problem putting it back in operation. During the years it was closed, UNRWA sent young Palestinians for training to centers elsewhere in Lebanon and in Jordan and Syria. After the Israelis left in August 1983, the school was taken over by the Progressive Socialist Party, Walid Jumblatt's Druze militia. UNRWA did not regain control until May 1985.

Before receiving authorization to reopen the school, de Jonge said, UNRWA had to reassure not only the Israelis but the Druze that it would not once again become a military academy for the PLO. One of the ironies of Lebanese politics is that Israelis and Syrians, Druze and Christians, even the Sunnis and Shias—whatever their feelings about one another—agree in wanting no more Palestinian military power in the south of Lebanon.

Siblin was in territory that Jumblatt's forces had captured from the Christian militia after the Israelis withdrew. Closely allied with Syria, the Druze had played a major role in the PLO's defeat in the war of the camps. De Jonge told me that UNRWA had to assure Jumblatt that the staff members who had made Siblin into a PLO boot camp would all be replaced. Siblin, he said, may still be a gleam in Arafat's eye but it is now totally nonpolitical—no posters, no graffiti, no slogans on the blackboards. The dorms, he said, still have pictures of Arafat on the wall, next to boxers and basketball players, but UNRWA will keep its vow that the school will be politically clean.

Finally, de Jonge said, UNRWA had to deal with the problem of missing equipment at Siblin. The Israeli army, he went on, had taken nearly all of the expensive machinery that the students needed for their courses. To restore the school, de Jonge said, UNRWA spent $1 million to replace equipment, and more remained to be purchased. The renovation is still not complete, he added, but Siblin reopened for classes in September 1987, and 400 students had already finished the first year of study. This year, he said, the student body has grown to about 700, and the school is almost in full operation.

In April 1989, the effort to restore Siblin was rewarded in a manner that UNRWA had not anticipated. The artillery war that opened in February between the forces of General Aoun in the Christian enclave and the Muslim alliance under the Syrians had made Beirut, for all practical purposes, uninhabitable. In March, all of UNRWA's schools in Beirut were closed. Finally, to save lives, Vienna ordered the field headquarters moved to Siblin, leaving behind only a few security men to safeguard property. On May 8, just a few hours after the last of the personnel departed, a near miss sent shrapnel through the windows of the building. At Siblin, de Jonge and his staff not only occupied office space but also made their lodgings in the dormitories of the training center. Since then, UNRWA's Lebanese operations have been administered from Siblin, with the understanding that de Jonge and the staff will return to Beirut whenever the shelling stops.

VI

UNRWA in Jordan

In Jordan, some 884,000 Palestinians carried UNRWA registration cards in 1988, a rise—thanks to an annual rate of population increase of 3.7 percent—from 716,000 at the beginning of the decade. About 60 percent of refugees who live outside Palestine are in Jordan.

It is conventionally estimated that more than half of Jordan's 3 million population—which counts only East Bank residents—is Palestinian, though some scholars place the proportion somewhat lower. The government does not publish an official figure, perhaps to avoid support of Israeli right-wingers who argue Israel's right to retain the West Bank on the grounds that Jordan is already a "Palestinian state." (The peace initiative of Prime Minister Yitzhak Shamir, approved by the Israeli cabinet on May 14, 1989, in fact, notes Israel's opposition to "creation of an *additional* Palestinian state in the Gaza district and in the area between Israel and Jordan. [Emphasis added].) According to UNRWA's calculations, Palestinians overall are 53 percent of Jordan's total and registered refugees nearly a third. Whatever figures are correct, the large Palestinian population imposes on UNRWA a more prominant role in the affairs of Jordan than of any other country.

Although largely a desert wasteland, Jordan be-

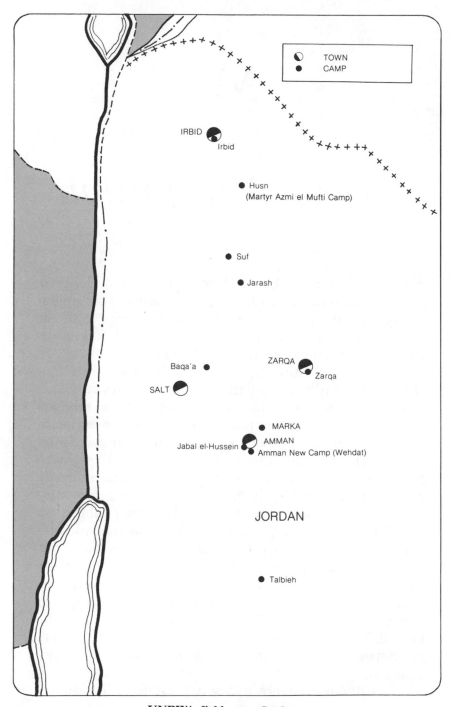

Legend:

◑ TOWN
● CAMP

IRBID ◑ Irbid

● Husn
(Martyr Azmi el Mufti Camp)

● Suf

● Jarash

Baqa'a ●

ZARQA ◑ Zarqa

SALT ◑

● MARKA

AMMAN
Jabal el-Hussein ● ● Amman New Camp (Wehdat)

JORDAN

● Talbieh

UNRWA field map: Jordan
Registered refugee population in Jordan: 870,490

Proportion of total registered refugee population: 38%

came remarkably prosperous during the 1970s, the years of the oil boom. It benefitted from direct subsidies from the governments of the oil-producing states but, not less important, from the industriousness of its Palestinian population. The Palestinians have been both producers and beneficiaries of Jordan's wealth. They established businesses, sent home hard currency from jobs held in the oil countries, and managed the investments of foreigners in Jordan. Given the tenuousness of its economy, Jordan has also counted heavily on UNRWA's annual expenditure within its borders. In 1988, UNRWA spent $65 million in Jordan, up from $52 million in 1983. Since the early 1980s, when oil prices dropped precipitously, Jordan has had to rely more than ever on UNRWA's dollars.

In some measure, Jordan's economic needs account for the vigorous fight that King Hussein's government long put up against UNRWA's decision to eliminate the basic rations program. It is not that any refugees were hungry. In fact, a lucrative racket long flourished in Jordan, in which "rations merchants" paid fees to refugees for use of their UNRWA identity cards, which they presented at distribution centers to obtain food to sell later on the black market. By eliminating the rations program, UNRWA put an end to the racket, but deprived Jordan of an ongoing economic benefit.

Jordan was near to losing much more of UNRWA's expenditures in 1981, when the agency's income had fallen so far behind needs that the commissioner-general threatened to close the school system throughout the region. UNRWA maintained in budget debates that such a decision had to be dictated by the agency's financial condition and nothing else. Jordan replied that any success UNRWA had in reducing its programs, even as part of a shift from lower to higher human priorities, took money out of the refugees' pockets. Jordan gloomily forecast that ending the rations was a step toward total abandonment of the UN's commitment to the refugees and fought ferociously to maintain the status quo.

Ultimately, however, the UN's political commitment is more important to the government of King Hussein than its economic aid. In management terms, it would be more efficient for the UN to write a check to Jordan for the sum that UNRWA spends in the country and allow the Jordanian government to run the schools, clinics, and other services that UNRWA performs. Economically, such an arrangement would even be to Jordan's advantage, but the Jordanian government is convinced that the presence of UNRWA, symbol of the international community's unfinished agenda, is vital to social stability.

"The Jordanians say that if UNRWA were dissolved, a half-million or a million Palestinians would be marching in the streets, and they might be correct about that," an agency official said to me. UNRWA's presence conveys to the Palestinians the impression—or the illusion—that the UN remembers that their destiny as residents in a foreign land is not fixed.

Without UNRWA, the refugees would have to integrate into Jordanian society, and Jordan would have no choice but to take them in. King Hussein has long acknowledged that, at least in principle, integration is not what the Palestinians want. But in the past few years of economic stringency, the native Jordanian population has conveyed unmistakable signs that it does not want integration either. The feeling of Jordanians that they have been imposed upon has been growing. Tolerance has been ebbing. A series of antigovernment demonstrations on the part of Jordanians in April 1989 seemed to convey, among its messages, a resentment of Palestinian economic competition, if not of the high priority the king has given to Palestinian political grievances in Jordanian diplomacy. The protests may well have been a harbinger of the instability that is likely to follow if Jordan is forced to absorb the Palestinians juridically into the state.

Yet, in practice, Jordanian policy has been precisely to integrate the Palestinians unreservedly into the Jordanian economy and with relatively few limitations into the Jordanian political structure. Though Palestinians retain unhappy memories of Jordan's rule in the years after 1948, in governing the West Bank, King Hussein came to think of them as his own people. Since losing the West Bank in 1967, the king has spared little effort to ease the pain inflicted on the local inhabitants by the Israeli occupation.

Palestinian-Jordanian relations fell to a low point in September 1970—"Black September" in Arab lore— when King Hussein sent in an army to suppress what appeared to be a clear effort by the PLO to overthrow his regime. It was a showdown that culminated three or four years of growing PLO power in Jordan, concentrated within the refugee camps. PLO headquarters was then in the New Amman camp on the outskirts of the city. Jordanians could enter only with PLO permission, and UNRWA could operate only by the PLO's leave. Though most refugees sympathized with the PLO, few endorsed its effort to bring down the state. Only a handful joined the organized PLO contingents during Black September. The king's army inflicted heavy casualties on the PLO's armed forces and drove them out of Jordan. Very few of the refugees decided to leave with them.

Notwithstanding this bloodshed, Jordan was the only Arab country that offered full citizenship to the refugees (the only exception made by Jordan was that of Palestinians with origins in the Gaza Strip, where they had been under Egyptian jurisdiction). Jordan opened its professions to the Palestinians, and offered their young people equal access to its public schools and universities. It welcomed in its towns and cities those Palestinians who chose to leave their homes in the camps. It gave Palestinians responsible posts in government and industry, and made funds available to them to invest in business.

With the increased well-being and the passage of years, the overt tensions between the Jordanian government and the PLO subsided. Enterprising Palestinians became the motor of Jordan's new prosperity and the Jordanians, richer themseves for this energy, seemed satisfied with the arrangement. When the Arab summit at Rabat in 1974 designated the PLO the "sole legitimate representative" of the Palestinian people, King Hussein—though unhappy at the rebuke by his fellow Arabs—graciously submitted.

Still, the PLO and the crown competed for Palestinian loyalties. Even as the evidence of a rising tide of support for the PLO in the West Bank grew, the king, with Israeli concurrence, continued to subsidize the vestiges of the bureaucracy that served him there before 1967. For years, the king scavenged for funds to implement a Jordan River Development Plan that included major improvements in the West Bank and Gaza. When talk turned to peace and the prospect of Israeli withdrawal, Hussein could be counted on to say the right things about PLO preeminence, but it was clear he foresaw playing a preponderant role in any Arab-Israeli negotiations with the aim of restoring Hashemite rule on both banks of the Jordan River.

For 20 years, King Hussein was in the forefront of the Arabs in the campaign to make peace with Israel based on the return of the West Bank and Gaza Strip. By the 1980s, he was ready to consent to a confederation of Jordan with a sovereign Palestine, and in 1985 he composed his differences with Yasir Arafat to make a joint peace proposal based on an international conference. In all of these efforts, he had the support of the Palestinians in his realm. In the end, he had nothing to show for his labors but a string of failures, and the Palestinians understood that if they were to get back the lost territories, it probably would not be through the ministrations of the Jordanian monarch.

Throughout these years, the king orchestrated a fine balance in the society. The secret police maintained a close but discreet watch over the refugee camps and the university campuses. The army, though seldom seen, was ever ready to defend internal tranquility. Though Palestinians held visible offices in the government, the most critical security posts in both the police and the army were held by Jordanians or by the few Palestinians of whose loyalty he was certain. Over the years, the king became increasingly sensitive to criticism of his policies, allowing the trappings of democracy to fade away, but Jordan never became oppressive like Syria or Iraq. The country, for the most part, remained relatively easy-going, with two communities, Jordanian and Palestinian, living side by side in reasonable harmony.

It was intrinsic to his policies that the king keep his personal image untarnished. He worked at it tirelessly. On the one hand, he took credit, quite legitimately, for being the Palestinians' benefactor. On the other hand, he took pains not to look as if he were trying to swallow the Palestinians. The royal family lived rather modestly; the regime suffered few scandals. The image the king conveyed was that of father to his people while generously leaving his children, Jordanian and Palestinian alike, free to identify themselves with different mothers.

The situation produced the irony of a government spending millions, particularly after 1983, to upgrade the refugee camps, often doing more for the Palestinians than they themselves wanted done. The king's munificence did not succeed—any more than a rising standard of living in Israel succeeded—in abating Palestinian nationalism. At best, it promoted stability, though the Palestinians barely acknowledged his efforts to improve their lives. I have heard stories of the Jordanian government *sneaking* piped water or street lights into a camp, such amenities having been vetoed by refugees who feared losing political credibility if their living conditions became too comfortable. More often, however, the government abandoned plans for improvements that were available to all citizens, but which camp inhabitants had resisted.

The government's leniency toward expressions of Palestinian nationalism set a tone for UNRWA. Under UN rules, UNRWA cannot tolerate overt political activity in its schools or in the youth activities centers that it operates in the camps. It cannnot risk a Siblin in Jordan, but it can nonetheless operate—far more easily than on the West Bank or in Gaza—within a framework that recognizes Palestinian nationalism as a reality.

"The Palestinian flag is a fact," said Per Olof Hallqvist, who was UNRWA's director in Amman when I visited in 1983 and who currently holds that post in Damascus. "I can't take the Palestinians' history away from them. According to the UN partition resolution of 1947, the promise of Palestine still exists in international law. I can try to stop the flaunting of guns and daggers, but I can't forbid them to plead their cause."

UNRWA's 4,300 teachers in Jordan, most of them young men and women with deeply held nationalist feelings, are a recurring problem to the agency. They are a permanent lobby on behalf of Palestinian nationhood, constantly pushing UNRWA to take positions of advocacy on behalf of Palestinian goals. They communicate their nationalism in the classroom, as UNRWA well knows, arousing students who for the most part have already been heavily politicized at home.

To an outsider like me, the result is apparent once inside the grounds of almost any UNRWA school. On their walls, painted by students, are murals rich in nostalgia for Palestine, free in depicting the symbolism of the struggle—flags, the Dome of the Rock in Jerusalem's Old City, commandos, maps, guns. Classes teach Palestinian folk arts, particularly the embroidery that Palestinian women wear on their gowns. I vividly recall a Palestinian folk celebration I witnessed in which children in the school yard lustily sang Palestinian folk songs and, with more enthusiasm than skill, danced Palestinian dances.

What the king's policy has done, however, is spare young Palestinians, no less than old, the duty of choice. Paradoxical as it may seem, most school-age refugees, even in identifying as Palestinians, think of themselves as Jordanian. They cheer for the PLO and are thrilled by the intifada, but it rarely occurs to them to enlist as fedayeen or cross the river to brave Israeli bullets. Much too young to have personal recollections of a Palestinian home, they would probably prefer remaining in Jordan to migrating to a newly established Palestinian state. Yet, young and old, they remain Palestinian in refusing to relegate to history's dustbin the dream of a return.

When the intifada started, the Jordanian government was uncertain as to how it would fare, given this obvious ambivalence within the Palestinian segment of its citizenry, the fragile balance of loyalties to Palestine and the PLO on the one hand and to Jordan and the king on the other. The Palestinians of the kingdom donated money to support of the intifada. They kept the telephone lines buzzing—with the relays established by long experience through friends in Europe or America—from Amman to the West Bank. The government was obviously nervous. It did not want the intifada to spread eastward. The Palestinians had stuck with the king during Black September in 1970. Would they stick with him still?

Determined not to be caught unawares, the Jordanian government stepped up surveillance of the Palestinian community, particularly inside the camps. It arrested a few political activists, though it held them only a month or two. It tightened restrictions on the camp visits of outsiders and insisted on monitoring conversations, even of UNRWA staff members. The Jordanian press, already tightly controlled, was reorganized and placed under even stricter discipline than before. Interestingly, there is evidence that the PLO bolstered Jordan's efforts by using its influence to keep the Palestinian community peaceful and maintain calm in the camps.

Ironically, in serving as the model for the antigovernment protests that shook the country in April, the intifada seems to have had more of a direct impact on Jordanians than on Palestinians in Jordan. In response to this unrest, the king appointed a new cabinet, promising more attention to the grievances of Jordanians. As these words are written, the king's position appeared secure. In the spring of 1989, with the intifada apparently confined to the west of the Jordan River, and the disorders to the east no longer a threat, he lifted some of the constraints imposed on the press. He also began encouraging talk of parliamentary elections, last held 21 years before.

By now, it seemed clear that King Hussein's gamble of July 31, 1988, had paid off—at least, in terms of domestic politics. That was the date on which the king surprised the world by announcing that he was formally cutting all of Jordan's ties with the West Bank, terminating a relationship that had began in 1948 but that over the years had become increasingly tenuous. Palestinians living in Jordan were henceforth to be considered permanently Jordanian, unless they chose to renounce citizenship. None did. West Bankers were to lose their citizenship and with it the right to establish residence in Jordan, although exceptions were to be made for health or family reasons. Nearly all subsidies to teachers and other officials were ended, though according to officials to whom I spoke in Amman, stipends continued to be paid to the wounded in the intifada and to the families of the dead. Talk on Jordanian television and in the press of links with the West Bank stopped abruptly, and the regulation of crossings of the Allenby Bridge became more rigorous.

Clearly, the PLO remained a worry for King Hussein. He had achieved a level of cordiality in dealing with it after so many decades of animosity, but he had failed to preempt it in the West Bank or to reach an accommodation with it on a joint policy for prospective peace negotiations. Surely, his reservations about holding parliamentary elections were based, at least in part, on the likelihood that the PLO would win a major victory. As it pressed on with its peace initiative, the PLO—to allay American fears of an independent Palestinian state—sought to persuade the king to agree publicly to federate the two sides of the Jordan River once a settlement with Israel was reached. But the king declined. He was particularly upset, having for 20 years led the effort to end the Israeli occupation, when the PLO's Arafat said he would now follow the lead in the peace process of Egypt's President Husni Mubarak.

Palestinians were at first shocked by the king's decision to sever his West Bank ties and grumbled that it had been taken without warning, but the grumbling was by no means a prelude to a surge of support for restoring the old bonds. Few Palestinians, in fact, even expressed regret. Early claims—heard more in Israel and the United States than among the Arabs or the Europeans—that the king's move was tactical and that nothing had really changed were refuted on the ground. When Jordanian actions confirmed over the ensuing months that the king meant what he had said, friend and foe alike acknowledged that the change had become part of a permanent new reality in the region.

UNRWA was not directly affected by the change. Administratively, the government signaled the transformation by abolishing the Ministry of Occupied Territories, which had been responsible since 1967 for conducting Jordan's West Bank relations, usually under the direction of a Palestinian as minister. In its place, the government established a Department of Palestinian Affairs within the Ministry of Foreign Affairs. UNRWA's daily dealings with Jordan were thus downgraded from the ministerial to the secretarial level, which is the level at which they are conducted in Syria, but neither the agency nor the refugees felt prejudiced by the shift. The PLO's delegation in Amman was raised to the ambassadorial level, and UNRWA found itself consulting occasionally with the PLO's Department of the Occupied Homeland, under the direction of Muhammad Milhem whom it knew as mayor of the West Bank town of Halhul, until his expulsion by the Israelis in 1979.

Since the change, all the parties—UNRWA, the government, the refugees—have gone about their business more or less as before, except for a feeling that the last word on the matter has not been spoken. King Hussein had broken the longstanding pattern in his relationship with the Palestinians, as well as with the Jordanians, and a new one was emerging only slowly.

Then, in the early summer of 1989, the government startled the skeptics by announcing that, in keeping with its pledge, it would conduct parliamentary elections in November. To be sure, political parties were not to be permitted, nor would a one-man-one-vote rule be invoked, but Palestinians—who would make up more than half the electorate—were to have a far greater share of the elected seats than they had held in the outgoing assembly. No one doubted, furthermore, that the PLO would have an important influence on the election's outcome. The new parliament, a source close to the king told me, would reflect the changes that had taken place in Jordan since the writing of the last constitution in 1951. The new representatives were expected, he said, to adopt a charter that would revise the nation's goals to include a more equitable sharing of power between the king and the people.

When I last visited Jordan in mid-summer 1989, the intifada was still raging, in spite of the increasingly harsh measures taken by the Israelis to contain it. The day to day fighting, along with the diplomatic maneuvering between Washington and Jerusalem, was still the focus of most Palestinians. The impending Jordanian political campaign had not yet captured popular attention, and I heard few predictions on how it would play itself out. Nonetheless, there was a pervasive awareness of the dynamism of events, and the unlikelihood that it could be stopped. Palestinians readily expressed the feeling that, much as the old status quo had already been transformed, even more significant changes were on the way.

VII

UNRWA in Syria

S yria, with 265,000 registered refugees, has fewer than any other UNRWA jurisdiction, less than a third the number that is in Jordan. More than 200,000 of the refugees live in Damascus, 10 percent of the capital's population. Most occupy the quarter called Yarmouk, a Palestinian suburb first settled after the 1948 flight, though swallowed up and digested long ago by Damascus' sprawl. Over four decades, Yarmouk has become a heavily populated working-class district, diverse in its living accommodations, bustling with shops, schools, movies, restaurants, offices, and workshops, fully integrated into the city itself.

In important ways, Syria has been kind to the refugees. It has opened its economy to them without discrimination, and many have prospered. Three basic limitations are imposed upon them: they cannot buy arable land, they cannot carry a Syrian passport, and they cannot own more than one house. Otherwise, it is agreed, they are treated in the economic realm no differently from Syrians.

"The refugees in Syria are no longer refugees," said Muhammad Nashashibi, a member of the PLO Executive Committee since 1972 and chairman of the PLO's economic department. Member of a distinguished Jerusalem

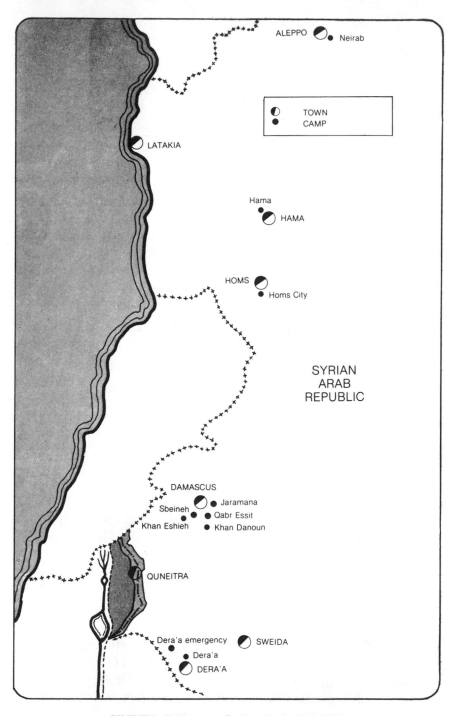

UNRWA field map: Syrian Arab Republic
Registered refugee population in Syrian Arab Republic: 265,221
Proportion of total registered refugee population: 12%

family, Nashashibi first arrived in Damascus in 1948. He lives comfortably with his family in a large apartment in the center of the city, but his movements are restricted. Damascus used to be a major center of the PLO, but its importance declined with the feud between Arafat and President Hafiz al-Asad in the early 1980s, and it remains the headquarters of only those Palestinian organizations hostile to Arafat's Fatah organization, depending on Syrian support. No longer a young man, Nashashibi rarely is allowed to leave the country. Faithful to the PLO mainstream, though distant from the centers of power, he continues his work as a researcher and planner into the Palestinians' future.

"Comparatively speaking, there is no unemployment among refugees," Nashashibi said. "Even in the camps, they almost all have jobs. The refugees have houses, work, income, education. They have done rather well in Syria. Those who are still in the camps live there as well as they did in their villages in Palestine. There may be political symbolism to staying in the camps, but that is not the reason they remain. Camp life has become reasonably comfortable and it is very cheap, so the refugees have no economic incentive to leave."

Politically, however, Palestinian life—in Syria as in Jordan—has been getting more difficult. Unlike Jordan, the intifada is not to blame; in Syria, it is President Asad's break with Arafat and his desire to have the refugees transfer their allegiance to Abu Musa, a PLO renegade whom Asad can control. For many years, Nashashibi recalled, Syria collected special taxes from Palestinians, which it turned over to the PLO for the struggle against Israel. It still collects the taxes, but now the money goes to the support of a Palestinian unit of the Syrian armed forces and thus back to the Syrian treasury. Abu Musa is also a beneficiary of these funds, but the Syrian contention that he is a legitimate alternative to the mainstream PLO has made no impact on the Palestinians. Abu Musa, it is said, cannot these days even stroll safely around Yarmouk.

Nashashibi said the Arafat problem has led Syria to tighten the surveillance of the secret police, a prominent element throughout Syrian society. Though a few known Arafat supporters have been imprisoned, the intrusion into everyday life is limited. Still, Palestinians are permitted no political activities, in fact no organizational activities of any kind. Most Palestinians obey their conditioned reflex by simply staying away from politics, even in casual talk. Palestinians are also subject to far more stringent rules than Syrians for leaving the country, with the only exception being the dissidents who are likely to make trouble for Arafat. The Palestinian community, Nashashibi said, used to be permitted celebrations for such holidays as "Land Day," but for any public assembly it now needs permission, which is never granted. Palestinians, proud as they are of it, handle even the intifada in a low-key way.

UNRWA has always had to contend in its work in Syria with the government's obsession with security. It is apparent that in each of its field offices, UNRWA's people work with a different set of expectations for which they adopt different operational responses. The UNRWA staff in Syria sees the government as paranoid and takes special pains to deal with Syria's ongoing presumption that everyone in the agency is a spy. The challenge is obviously less of a burden than the physical dangers of Lebanon or the Gaza Strip, but it nonetheless creates tensions that are wearing to the spirit.

UNRWA's teachers, for example, are regularly arrested, although as UN employees they are supposed to be "functionally immune," which means they should have protection from arrest for on-duty conduct. UNRWA pleads a right to have all arrests reported to it promptly, with explanations, but the results are uneven. Routinely, UNRWA protests high-handedness to the Ministry of Foreign Affairs, relying on the professional commitment of trained diplomats to recognized international procedures, but the reply is often that responsibility for this arrest or that belongs to the *mukhabarat*, the security police, a law unto itself. In Syria, it is taken for granted that everyone, including ministers, is frightened of the security services.

The government's chief instrument of supervision over UNRWA is a bureau known to all as GAPAR, the acronym for General Authority for Palestine Arab Refugees. Administratively, it is part of the Ministry of Labor and Social Affairs, but it functions with considerable autonomy. Except for the police, which are under the Ministry of Interior, it runs the camps through a Palestinian staff. UNRWA staff members expend much energy calculating how to deal most effectively with the unpredictability of the Syrians. GAPAR, their day-to-day contact with the government, is where they conventionally start.

"In the past, some UNRWA directors have used a consistent, confrontational strategy," said Robert Gallagher, who was head of the UNRWA office when I visited in 1983. "I have tried not to confront GAPAR or the ministries on small matters, but only on big ones, which enable me to skip the bureaucrats and go directly to the decision makers. I've adopted the theory that it's easier to get a favorable decision at a higher, rather than a lower, level. And sometimes it works."

On my 1989 visit to Damascus, a veteran UNRWA hand gave me a slightly different view. "Dealing with the Israelis," he said, "is straight, sharp, even harsh. Here it is more oriental, more indirect. If we have to get something done, we have to go through many formal courtesies. We don't barge in. We can't be dogmatic or talk about our rights. First, we make personal contact and try to reach agreement privately. Then, we write the formal letters, making sure they contain no surprises. Using these tactics, we generally get cooperation from the state."

The same staff member told me, as an example, that when London broke diplomatic relations with Syria over a terrorist incident late in 1986, UNRWA feared the government, in reprisal, would expel the British nationals who served the agency in Damascus. The office, committed to defend the rights of international civil servants, braced for an encounter, but GAPAR, to UNRWA's delight, announced sweetly that it would not mix the two worlds of bilateral and UN relations, and the British remained.

In 1988, as another example, GAPAR helped UNRWA solve a serious problem involving a shipment of flour—a gift of Japan but purchased in the United States—that arrived riddled with weevils. To save the shipment, UNRWA needed to have the flour remilled. The agency went to GAPAR, which agreed to take up the matter with the Ministry of Supply and Planning and the Ministry of Foreign Affairs. Ten days later, GAPAR announced that the government would trade the tainted for clean flour, taking only a modest fee to cover its remilling costs. Again, UNRWA was thrilled.

GAPAR does, however, monitor UNRWA relentlessly. The agency's Damascus office knows that at every level it is staffed by GAPAR informers. Often it knows who they are but, as a practical matter, cannot fire them. In fact, it sometimes uses them for communicating informally with the government because they are generally quicker than official channels.

The system is brutal to staff morale. Internationals are given regular leave to get away from the tension, but local employees rarely have that luxury, and their situation is rendered more difficult by the suspicion with which the government perceives all Palestinians. To the mukhabarat, any Palestinian is an Arafat supporter, which, in fact, most are. The suspicion keeps the community on edge, which is part of its aim. It aggravates divisions that already exist among Palestinians and makes the job of the security services a bit easier.

When I visited the GAPAR office in 1983, Subhi Abu Khalil, who was then the general-director, made no apology for the government's surveillance system. The Asad-Arafat feud was then in its early stages, and Abu Khalil denied that the Palestinians were in any way singled out. "We have a heavy security apparatus in the camps and in the refugee communities," he said, "as we have in the entire country." Since then, the screws applied to the Palestinians, as one UNRWA staff member put it, "have been tightened about a quarter-turn."

In fact, despite a history of strained relations, Syria never experienced anything like Jordan's pre-1970 troubles with the PLO or a bloody episode like Black September. The explanation surely does not lie in Syria's benevolence. Syria has not hesitated to kill thousands of Palestinians in the refugee camps of Lebanon or, for that matter, thousands of Syrians, as it did in the 1982 uprising of the Muslim Brotherhood in Hama. More central to Syria's confidence is the relatively small size of the Palestinian population that—in contrast to the Palestinians in Jordan—precludes its being a threat to the state. Significantly, neither in 1982 nor during the repeated shellings of the Palestinian camps in Lebanon has the refugee community shown the slightest disposition to respond to calls to join an anti-Syrian front.

The closest the Palestinians have come may have been in the fall of 1983, when Abu Musa's forces were attacking PLO loyalists near Tripoli and Palestinians in Yarmouk took to demonstrating in the street. Some of the demonstrating, it seems, was directed against Abu Musa, some against Arafat, and some against the action of the Syrian government. None of it was very angry, and most of Yarmouk's population kept its distance anyway. Shopkeepers pulled down their shutters and went home; schools, both UNRWA's and the government's, suspended classes. Notwithstanding, Syrian armed forces stepped in after a day and, though reports were confusing, 20 or 30 refugees were believed killed in gunfire. Characteristically, the government was silent about the episode, though obviously order was restored.

The relative passivity of the Palestinians surely does not mean, whatever the Syrian government would prefer, that they have given up their attachment to Arafat and the PLO. The funeral in Yarmouk of Abu Jihad—*nom de guerre* of Arafat's deputy, Khalil al-Wazir, who was murdered in Tunis by an Israeli assault team—became the occasion in April 1989 for a tumultuous pro-PLO outburst by the Palestinians. The Syrians at that time were talking about returning to the good graces of the Arabs after their embrace of Khomeini during the Iran-Iraq war. A reconciliation with the PLO looked like a good place to start. It is within that context that they decided to let Palestinians march in Abu Jihad's funeral, though, in fact, reconciliation with neither Arafat nor the Arab world has yet taken place.

For the Syrian government, UNRWA—certainly not the PLO—is the Palestinians' representative. GAPAR apparently had some second thoughts after the killings in Yarmouk in 1983, for example, and to placate the refugees granted to UNRWA a series of permits to facilitate repairs and construction in the camps that had long been delayed. It would never occur to the Syrian government that allowing the refugees to organize to represent their own interests might promote stability. Such an idea would be foreign to the region. Syria, however, is comfortable—and so are the Palestinians—having UNRWA, a disinterested party, represent these interests in the refugees' behalf.

"UNRWA has always been a humanitarian institution," said Per Olof Hallqvist, who in 1988 became the UNRWA director in Damascus. "We've done no institution-building here. UNRWA has an administrative structure. The PLO has a political structure. Unfortunately, the refugees have no structure at all. UNRWA has trained teachers, administrators, doctors, managers, all to work within our structure. We've never taught them to establish a structure of their own. That has simply been outside our mandate."

In conversations, GAPAR consistently takes a hard line on the politics of UNRWA's programs, as do the Syrian delegates in annual UNRWA budget debates at the United Nations. GAPAR complains that UNRWA's economies—particularly the termination of the basic rations program—have imposed heavy financial burdens on Syria, running into many millions of dollars a year. It complains that UNRWA's spending for emergency relief in Lebanon and, more recently, in the West Bank and Gaza has shortchanged the ongoing needs of Syria. GAPAR blames the shortfall on a "political deficit," refusing to concede a real lack of funds.

"UNRWA always claims it has money problems, which keep it from doing what it would like to do," said Muhammad Abu Zarad, the director-general of GAPAR. Abu Zarad is himself a Palestinian refugee as all the heads of GAPAR have been since 1964. "UNRWA argues that the budget depends on external factors, that the donors have a large control over expenditures. That should not be allowed because of the adverse effects on refugees. So many services have been curtailed. UNRWA used to take full responsibility for the camps—water, paving roads, trash collections. Now it does much less. It used to provide rations to 100,000 refugees in Syria, and now the number is down to 20,000. UNRWA used to provide books, paper and pencils to its students, but that's suspended, too.

"This has a bad effect on refugees, especially since economic conditions in Syria are not good. UNRWA uses the pretext of emergencies in Lebanon and the occupied territories to limit services, but these programs should not be conducted at the expense of the refugees here. The refugees cannot be held responsible for UNRWA's deficit. That is UNRWA's responsibility.

"GAPAR tries its best to provide a good life to the Palestinians with the budget assigned to it by the government, but Syria is bearing extravagant costs. UNRWA, for example, provides only nine years of schooling. We supply kindergartens and, after the preparatory years, the refugees enroll in a government school and, later, in a government university. That runs into millions of Syrian pounds."

Abu Zarad gave me an estimate of 600 million Syrian pounds—about $55 million at the official rate, $15 million at the international market rate—that Syria spends for the refugees. UNRWA documents confirmed his figures. GAPAR's official position, stated to me by Abu Zarad's predecessor in 1983, is "that the Syrian government has nothing to benefit from UNRWA. The funds go only to the refugees." But that statement was more than a shade disingenuous.

Abu Zarad's calculations failed to take into account that Palestinians, called upon to fulfill the same military and social duties as Syrians, are also assessed the same level of taxes—more, in fact, if one adds the levies that once went to the PLO and now go to the treasury. UNRWA, meanwhile, pays for schools for more than 53,000 refugee children as well as for other services that the government routinely furnishes. A strong argument can be made—applicable not just to Syria—that UNRWA, far from fleecing the "host" countries, as GAPAR's complaints imply, actually provides them with substantial annual subsidies. Like Jordan and Israel, Syria has serious financial problems. Some experts say it is nearly bankrupt. From that perspective, what UNRWA spends is important not only to the Palestinians but also to the Syrians.

"UNRWA is bringing in $20 million in hard-currency expenditures this year," Hallqvist said, "and is budgeted to bring in $23 million next year. For what we get, that's more than we should spend, but the Syrian pound, though devalued slightly last January, is still very much overpriced. That discourages us from investing in capital projects. But considering the small proportion of the population the refugees represent, and the fact that most of them are self-sustaining, $20 million is a major infusion of capital."

Syria has not stopped complaining about UNRWA's termination of the general rations program in 1983. When the special hardship program was instituted in its place, GAPAR threatened UNRWA with the arrest of any employees engaged in its implementation. Repeating the standard Arab argument, Syria insisted that all refugees were "hardship" cases. It also said the program was divisive, and that UNRWA had no right to investigate refugees for hardship or anything else. When the government announced to the Damascus director that it would expel him if the program continued, UNRWA beat a tactical retreat. But a few weeks later, Commissioner-General Olof Rydbeck arrived from Vienna, and he applied the theory that the higher the level of talks, the better the chance of success. Rydbeck met a range of top government officials and, on his departure, UNRWA resumed the hardship program. It never received official approval, however; the government simply made no further protests.

"Still, the Syrians won't let go on the special hardship issue," Hallqvist continued. "They're always talking about it. One of the reasons is that they object strongly to our checking the refugees for their qualifications to receive rations. They want to give us a list of the hardship cases, and we won't agree to that. So they allow us to investigate on paper but not to conduct home visits. They claim UNRWA is spying, and you know how deeply they feel about that.

"The Syrian government was very upset when Commissioner-General Giacomelli said last summer that UNRWA had to give financial priority to the new needs in the occupied territories. That's where our donors—including the Arab states, which barely contributed in the past—want us to put the money. In a sense, even Lebanon is being shortchanged. I don't blame the Syrians, but they resent that, relatively, so much is going to the intifada and so little is coming here."

Abu Zarad would not answer when I asked him what impact the conflict between Syria and the PLO had on the refugees, referring me with a laugh to the Foreign Ministry for an answer. He did, however, indicate that Syria still held to the position that neither the Arab countries nor the communist bloc had any responsibility for remedying UNRWA's budget shortages. Syria contends that the refugee problem is the product of Western colonialism, and that the colonial powers alone should pay for it. Similarly, he rejected the argument made by some that the Palestinian situation should be joined with other refugee problems in the UN's Office of the High Commissioner for Refugees.

"UNRWA was established by the United Nations," Abu Khalil said to me six years ago, "in recognition of the crime committed by the major Western powers against the entire Palestinian people. A whole people was thrown off their land and a new state set up within their country. This situation is not just unique in our time. It is unique in history. UNRWA exists to ensure the rectification of this injustice."

Nashashibi, the Jerusalemite who reflects the thinking of the mainstream PLO, set a more modest standard and evaluated UNRWA's performance more generously. "UNRWA has rendered good service to the Palestinians," he said. "We criticize them for reducing their support. We criticize them for keeping their head office in Vienna when we think it should be in Damascus or Amman. We want them to press for higher budgets rather than tolerate cuts. But whether it's in Israel or the Arab countries, UNRWA watches out for the best interests of the Palestinians. We trust them and are grateful to them."

VIII

UNRWA in the Future

For 40 years, the United Nations nurtured the notion that UNRWA was a temporary agency. Every three years, its mandate had to be renewed by a vote of the General Assembly. Yet no one, since the early days, talked seriously of ending it. On the other hand, very few talked of making it permanent. The paradox is intrinsic to the Arab-Israeli conflict.

"We'll remain a politically jerry-built organization forever," Commissioner-General Rydbeck said to me in 1983, "because making UNRWA permanent would be an admission by the international community that there is no solution to the Middle East struggle. It would be politically impossible to amend the UNRWA statute to incorporate the agency, for example, into the UN bureaucracy. But yet, there's no prospect of terminating UNRWA's mandate. The Palestinian issue is so basic to the Middle East conflict that any effort to change UNRWA would open the doors to a debate on every aspect of the Arab-Israeli relationship, and bring the Big Powers in with it. The debate would be a Pandora's box, and who knows where it would end? No one wants that.

"While our responsibilities have taken on a permanent character, our mandate makes us temporary in our psychology. If we at times seem to lack direction, to drift, the explanation is that there is no agreement in the international community on what our goals should be."

One mark that unquestionably sullies UNRWA's record—as Rydbeck, and every other commissioner-general, including Giacomelli, would no doubt admit—has been its failure to train the Palestinians in any significant way for the demands of self-government. Rydbeck acknowledged to me in 1983 that UNRWA made too many decisions for the Palestinians, depriving them of the training to make decisions for themselves. He called it UNRWA's "paternalism," and he said he did not know what to do about it.

"We don't have so much as a PTA in an UNRWA school," he said. "We've tried to get the parents involved in the problems of the schools, but we've had only limited success. The Palestinians think of the schools as UNRWA's schools, not their schools. They are not accustomed to community responsibility, and we don't know how to instill it in them."

The Israelis tried setting up councils in the refugee camps on the West Bank, as well as in some of the towns and villages, but their aim, far from being self-government, was to serve the ends of the military administration. The Palestinians looked upon these councils as quisling organizations, and UNRWA's office in Jerusalem actually protested their establishment.

The shaping of Palestinian leadership was resisted not only by the Israelis, however. Jordan and Syria were no more tolerant in endorsing the formation of groups that seemed likely, at some future time, to claim some measure of political independence. Syria even resisted establishment of advisory bodies for such self-help projects in the camps as street-paving or sewers. It is hard to imagine that UNRWA, no matter how hard it pushed, would have been permitted by any one of the host governments to organize "community development" projects, as, say, the US Peace Corps does to promote self-reliance in villages of the Third World. In its domains, the UNRWA staff—more often the internationals than the locals—has had to make even the simplest decisions.

"Self-government for the Palestinians is important," Rydbeck said, "but it obviously is not a job for us. We have to follow the mandate of the General Assembly, and it is narrow. Vocational and teacher training, advancement to higher studies, that is our work. We have to think of them as building-blocks, rather than get into politics itself."

It is only since the intifada, and the giddy hopes accompanying it for an Israeli-Palestinian settlement, that talk has begun on a future that is different from the four decades of UNRWA's past. The talk focuses not so much on abolishing UNRWA, though for the first time that seems ultimately possible, but on the role that the agency might play in the transition between war and peace. Not even the most fiery nationalists have, within my hearing, ever claimed that the Palestinians are ready to run a government. Slowly, a consensus seems to be building that UNRWA's experience and good name are assets that will be badly needed as a new era replaces the old.

To understand the current Israeli position on UNRWA's prospective role, it is necessary to go back to a program that emerged in the 1980s and had attached to it the name of Mordechai Ben-Porat, who chaired a committee on refugee resettlement while serving as minister without portfolio in the Begin government. Like many Israelis, Ben-Porat argued against the official UN position that fairness to the refugees required their repatriation or, at least, their compensation for lost property. The Ben-Porat plan was based on the theory of resettlement of the refugees in the society at large, thereby terminating the refugee status of those who fled from their homes as a result of the Arab-Israeli wars. The plan claimed justification in Israel's settlement of some 600,000 Jews who arrived as refugees from Arab lands. It was Ben-Porat's contention that resettlement of the Palestinians would formalize an exchange of population that had been consummated in 1948 and the years that immediately followed. The Ben-Porat plan proposed to break up the camps of the West Bank and the Gaza Strip and resettle their inhabitants, on a voluntary basis, in decent housing in the towns and cities. By implication, Israel would be setting a precedent for absorption that its Arab neighbors might one day be expected to follow. Ben-Porat was careful to say, however, that Israel was making the proposal without prejudice to any future Arab-Israeli political negotiations. Ben-Porat insisted that his ideas were both humanitarian and nonpolitical, though he admitted to the hope—despite historical evidence of its futility—that better living standards would divert the Palestinians from nationalist goals.

Officially UNRWA, as an administrative body, took no position of its own on the Ben-Porat plan. The refugees themselves unequivocally rejected the idea, and in 1983 the Arab states persuaded the UN General Assembly to denounce the Israeli idea as "a violation of (the refugees') inalienable right of return." Although UNRWA found something tempting in the prospect of better living standards, it faced pressure from its clients. UNRWA hedged, and finally issued a statement which did not disclaim all sympathy for the Israeli proposal, but opposed it on grounds that the United Nations could not consent to "any attempt to coerce refugees into compliance."

Notwithstanding the UN vote, Israel moved toward a realization of Ben-Porat's program. It had, in fact, been following the principles since 1971, when it first built a housing project in the Gaza Strip and invited the poorest inhabitants of the camps to move in. The PLO at the time forbade the refugees to accept the offer, and for more than a year no families did. Within UNRWA, however, the housing projects were seen as a step up for the refugees, and there was some tacit approval of what the Israelis were doing.

The difference that Ben-Porat brought to Israel's ongoing policy was one of magnitude. Ben-Porat talked of a figure of $1.5 billion to build houses, not including the costs of administration or land acquisition. He tried to get the money from the Americans, and when they made clear that they were not interested, the plan as official policy died. Israel's commitment to resettlement remained, however, and the migration from the camps into Israeli housing—though limited to a few hundred families a year—has continued to this day. Since the policy was instituted, some 70,000 refugees have moved from the Gaza camps into better homes nearby.

The intifada did not nullify Israel's faith in the idea of the Ben-Porat plan, though in practice the Israeli government had widened the concept from housing to address the standard of living generally in the occupied territories and particularly in the camps. Brigadier General Fredy Zach returned repeatedly to this objective in our talk in the Hakirya, Israel's "Pentagon" in downtown Tel-Aviv. Zach, an athletic-looking man of 42, holds the title of deputy coordinator for Judea-Samaria and the Gaza District; in this capacity, he watches over UNRWA for the Israeli government. In the course of an interview, Zach talked at length of the prospects for investments by UNRWA, along with other public and private international bodies, to improve the conditions in which the refugees live under the army's rule.

"We have no problems with UNRWA," Zach said. "The role it plays in the intifada is basically humanitarian, and we will not interfere. UNRWA provides services that we do not. It's doing a job that is important to us.

"What we would like is for UNRWA to become more involved in the daily life of the camps by increasing its investments in roads, sewerage, housing. The Israeli government has increased its concern in the last four or five years, largely at the urging of George Shultz when he was the American secretary of state, for what he called the 'quality of life' in the territories. Our means, however, are limited, and so we encourage UNRWA to help us. When the Palestinians have something to lose, they will think twice about terror. The army's policy is to try to decrease terror by improving services. We have stayed on the course Shultz proposed, even with the intifada."

UNRWA has remained faithful to its history in sharing the concern expressed by the Israelis—though not necessarily the motives—about living conditions in the camps. A higher living standard, they maintained, would neither deprive Palestinians of their identity nor divert them from their nationalist goals. As one Palestinian commented, "Even if you move us to palaces, the real historical, political, national problem will remain." In speaking of Israeli resettlement efforts, another Palestinian quipped that the refugees who moved from the camps into the housing projects, far from being integrated into a new society, simply brought their old camp mentality to a different place. UNRWA, anxious not to discourage a migration to better conditions, said officially about the Israeli offer that it would not oppose measures "voluntarily accepted by the refugees."

Taking account of the intifada, UNRWA's commissioner-general, in his annual report to the General Assembly for 1987-88, referred to the "difficult conditions under which the refugees were living, especially those in the Gaza Strip," noting that these conditions contributed to the "bitterness and despair" that led to the uprising. "After the uprising began," Giacomelli said in his talk with me, "I spoke to representatives of the refugees, and they liked the idea of a construction program, provided it was done by UNRWA and not the Israelis, and was not a cover for the Ben-Porat plan, meaning that it did not imply resettlement."

In early 1988, shortly after the intifada started, the agency drafted a three-year, $65 million program of capital investment and, in the spring, introduced it at a meeting with donor countries. UNRWA quickly obtained $10 million in pledges for the program. At the same time, the agency stepped up its own building of new schools, clinics, and other infrastructural facilities, though lack of funds limited the effort to a program, Giacomelli wrote, that "necessarily fell short of what refugees living in the territories were seeking." It was apparent UNRWA would need much more to make any real improvement in camp life.

"I met with the major donor countries and I was even invited to Tunis to address the Council of Ministers of the Arab League," Giacomelli told me. "I told them all that the spark of the intifada was the miserable living conditions in Gaza, which the curfews, strikes, and the constant military presence have made only worse. Obviously, the needs were longstanding but, as I saw it, this was the moment to reach the donors when they were at their most receptive. I promised that UNRWA would keep relief at a minimum, designating its funds, as much as possible, to sewers, water lines, and buildings, in the hope that this would give the refugees more patience and endurance. The Arab countries responded more positively than I ever dreamed, pledging more than $20 million for relief and projects. Even the PLO donated money. The intifada gave the international community the advantage of hindsight. Its reaction was to be more forthcoming."

Giacomelli indignantly rejected any suggestion that UNRWA, in proposing the special building program, was playing the game of the Israelis.

"If Israel wants to interpret it as an effort on our part to contain the intifada," he said, "it can do as it wishes. But UNRWA's motivation in proposing this program was quite different. Even if we wanted to, it is beyond our capacity to slow the intifada. Our program is not what the Israelis had in mind—if only because of the magnitude. They were contemplating $1.5 or $2 billion for the Ben-Porat plan which is what Mr. Shamir requested for the territories when he was last in Washington. Our plan is for $65 million which is a drop in the bucket. We're glad the Israelis approve of our investment in the camps, but our program has no political implications. It is a gesture to make life for the refugees a bit more bearable. Unfortunately, it is all we can afford, so it is just a gesture."

Muhammad Nashashibi, chairman of the PLO's economic department, talked to me in Damascus of his vision for UNRWA's future. Ironically, in calling upon the agency for increased investment in the West Bank and the Gaza Strip, it resembled what General Zach conveyed to me of Israel's wishes, but Nashashibi's vision started from the quite different premise of imminent Israeli withdrawal. Nashashibi looked to UNRWA as an instrument in the transition of the West Bank and the Gaza Strip from occupied territory to independent state.

"You remember," Nashashibi said to me, "that there was once an active 'W' in UNRWA's name—a 'W' which fell into disrepute and disuse as long ago as 1951. The 'W' stands for Works, and it was part of UNRWA's original mandate. I propose that it be rehabilitated and restored to use. That could be very important in giving the new state a promising start.

"The PLO would like to cooperate with UNRWA, along with other UN organizations, to select certain projects and recruit international assistance. The PLO has $100 million at its disposal through Arab support, contingent upon the UN's coming up with an equal amount. We would like to use that money to absorb into the economy of the state the Palestinians from the occupied territories who are now working in Israel. We calculate the numbers at 18,000 in agriculture, 14,000 in industry, and 55,000 in construction. Israel currently has a positive balance of trade of $500 million annually with the occupied territories—that is, it exports $800 million and imports $300 million. The territories are Israel's second largest market, after the United States. Obviously, there will have to be some adjustments here, either to provide import substitution or export potential.

"We also have major work to do in housing. According to Israel's Central Bureau of Statistics, people are living six to a room in Gaza, slightly less in the West Bank. We will have to build many houses, as well as rebuild those that were destoyed by the Israelis. I think the refugee camps will have to be demolished. [Libya's Colonel Muammar] Qadhafi promises to help on housing funds. But our highest priority must still be productive investment in agriculture and industry.

"One thing we cannot tell is how many Palestinians will return to the new state. Because there has been so much moving around, we even don't know how many refugees there are, or where they are. UNRWA's figures on population in the camps are not reliable. I would expect a return of 50,000 from Syria, perhaps 200,000 from Lebanon and a few thousand from the Gulf and Egypt. I don't see many at all coming from Jordan.

"Any peace negotiations will also produce a struggle on the issue of compensation to the refugees. Compensation, as part of the right of return, is not something the PLO will be able to deal with, as the Israeli government dealt with compensation from Germany after World War II. I think the issue will have to be resolved on a family by family basis, and many families may refuse to accept compensation from Israel at all. Some may simply renounce it, if that is what they must do to keep their right of return alive. The compensation funds could be an important asset in building the new state.

"But whatever the numbers, UNRWA will have a major role to play. We will count on it to mobilize international support for us. We will need UNRWA for some time to come."

Nabil Sha'ath has the title of chairman of the political committee of the Palestine National Council, which is the parliamentary body of the PLO. His influence within PLO circles, however, stems more from a relationship of friend and adviser to Yasir Arafat. An American-educated intellectual, Sha'ath epitomizes the steady shift of the PLO from a resistance organization waging "armed struggle" against Israel to a political organization committed to establishing peace and building a state.

Sha'ath has also taken responsibility for planning the future of the Palestinian state. His role, no doubt, overlaps Nashashibi's in Damascus, but in working out of Cairo, he is much freer, and he has ready access not only to the PLO leadership but also, he said, to Gazans and West Bankers who move easily in and out of Israel. Sha'ath, whom I interviewed during one of his frequent visits to the United States, told me he has assigned teams to study land and water use in the new state, as well as needs in agriculture and industry, health and social services, education and foreign trade.

"We operate on the assumption," he said, "that there will be an independent Palestinian state by 1994. Another assumption is that we will have a million Palestinians from the outside to absorb, giving us, by our calculations, a population of 3.5 million by the end of the century. It is also our assumption that we will get back most of the water and land of the occupied territories, giving us room for expansion of agriculture and industry, especially in the Jordan Valley. Still, it is unlikely we will be self-sufficient in food production. That is one reason for still another assumption—that we must build a modern port in the city of Gaza.

"Our objective is to create a high productivity, high tech, export-driven economy, offering services like research centers and hospitals, construction and insurance companies, banks and other activities that Palestinians have done well with on the outside. We would like the new state to be a Middle East Singapore—certainly not another sleepy Yemen—with a competitive, non-polluting economic system based on private enterprise and with the government in a supportive role. We will not have enough water or land for heavy industry. We prefer small-scale, specialized industries—in computers, communications, book publishing, and biogenetics, maybe even in diamond cutting and polishing which we have learned from the Israelis.

"We're not too worried about money. Most of the capital will come from Palestinians living abroad, as well as from the Arab countries. We have broad commitments from Japan and the Europeans. The United States will surely make a pledge in the interest of stability and prosperity in the region. We will need billions to prepare for the returning refugees, but we think the money will be there when we need it."

Sha'ath spoke eloquently about the democracy by which the new state would be governed. Palestinians, he said, had for too long been the victims of repression, not just in the occupied territories but in the Arab countries, ever to create a repressive state of their own. He insisted that the state would have multiparty politics, free speech, local elective bodies, a criminal code without political crimes, and no secret police. Both communists and Islamic fundamentalists will be free to establish their own parties, he said, but the use of force will be illegal across-the-board in the political system.

Sha'ath criticized UNRWA for taking so long to begin consulting with the PLO on the problems of the Palestinians. For decades, he said, UNRWA generated resentment among the Palestinians, who saw it as an agent for humiliating them with charity while it white-washed the international community. Only after 1974, when the PLO obtained observer status at the United Nations, did UNRWA begin to identify its goals with those of the organization, and a rapprochement with the Palestinians followed. Since then, the animosity has vanished, he said, and UNRWA now has won the confidence of the entire Palestinian community.

"We in the PLO would like to engage in joint planning with UNRWA when the decision on establishing the state is made," Sha'ath said. "It is our view that UNRWA will have to continue its work for the first five years of our independence, maintaining the operation of its schools and hospitals. During this period, UNRWA will train cadres to run these institutions, and also make its facilities and skills available to help the refugees coming in from outside. Gradually, its schools and hospitals will be turned over to the government, and UNRWA's operations will dissolve into the Ministry of Health, the Ministry of Refugee Affairs and the Ministry of Education. Since the intifada, Palestinians have come to love UNRWA, and they trust it to help bring the new state to where it is self-reliant."

Giacomelli, in his talks with me, expressed many of the same ideas as Sha'ath and Nashashibi. His aggressive view of UNRWA's responsibilities for the future stood in sharp contrast to those his predecessor expressed to me in 1983, before the intifada broke the political logjam, before a sense of dynamism replaced the resignation that nothing would ever change in the Middle East. At that time, Commissioner-General Rydback told me that UNRWA had undertaken no studies on how to solve the refugee problem or made long-term appraisals of where the agency was going. In contrast, Giacomelli, seizing on the opportunities presented by fast-moving political changes seemed restrained only by the need to avoid the impression that UNRWA was overreaching or planning to usurp the powers of other international service agencies.

"We have a duty to offer our services to the peace process," Giacomelli said, "and to what comes after peace is achieved. But we have to be cautious in not sending out the wrong signals. We have to be flexible, stay in a state of high training, then decide when the time is ripe to change our approach. Since we have some credibility with both sides, maybe it is our duty to make some proposals. We have talked in the agency about whether the international community does not have the right to expect that we will come up with ideas, not just administrative ideas but political ideas. But we have to make sure the time is right."

On March 21, 1989, Giacomelli, with the endorsement of the UN secretary-general, took the initiative of calling a meeting in Vienna of representatives of all the United Nations agencies that might have a role to play in assisting a new Palestinian state. Under rules set by Israel, UNRWA and the United Nations Development Program (UNDP) are the only UN organizations currently permitted access to the territories. The others have had no direct experience there or even the means of acquiring the data needed for work. Present at the two-day meeting, in addition to UNRWA and UNDP, were representatives of WHO, UNESCO, UNICEF, the UN Population Fund, the

World Food Program, the International Labor Organization, and the UN Environmental Program. In all, 17 UN agencies sent delegations.

Giacomelli described the meeting to me as a low-profile session, an exchange of views on how the agencies could help each other in delivering vital services. The timing was right, he said, and all the delegates brought a positive attitude to the prospect of being ready whenever the Israeli army withdrew. It was agreed that informal working groups would be set up to explore the local potential in such areas of concern as health and education, employment and industry, housing and the environment. UNRWA's duty, he said, was to serve as the umbrella, both before and after a political settlement. Giacomelli invited the excluded agencies to send survey teams under UNRWA's aegis whenever they chose and promised that UNRWA would be prepared to coordinate the work of whatever UN agencies offer their services after the occupation ends.

"As I see it," Giacomelli said, "for the transition period to a Palestinian state, the PLO would be the potential government, the UN bodies the executive agencies, and the international community would provide the money. UNRWA has one great asset the other bodies do not have: we have trained Palestinians in our ranks. Our Palestinian staff has been tried in difficult circumstances and, on the whole, its performance has been very good. These people will bring to the state considerable expertise in administration, in process.

"The transition must provide the time to build administrative structures, without which the new state cannot survive. The Palestinians on our staff will play the principal role; the internationals will provide some guidance but play a lesser role. We in UNRWA, being careful not to step on toes, can feed our skills and those of the other agencies into the new government.

"Maybe the new government will be the PLO. Maybe, if there is a Palestinian election, some authorized body will want to take over some of our functions. We'll be delighted. The sooner we go out of business the better. We'll hand over our work, in whole or in pieces, to whatever Palestinian authority we are told. It will be a happy day for UNRWA to close shop, and happy for me when I am discharged of my duties by the General Assembly. I know that we are looking into the unknown. The reality may work itself out quite differently from all this. But sometimes, you know, we have a duty to look into the crystal ball—at least a little. It would be a mistake if we did not."

Index

Abu Jihad: PLO and Syria, 101–102
Abu Musa: PLO and Syria, 97
Abu Zarad, Muhammad: UNRWA
  and Syria, 103–104
Arab states: economic development,
  38–39;
  UNRWA staff, 48;
  refugee registration, 50;
  UNRWA contributions, 58
Army, Israeli: conduct, 1, 4, 17–18;
  schools, 15–16;
  West Bank, 16–17;
  RAOs, 26, 27–28;
  Lebanon, 71

Backer, Zacharias: military
  administration, 17–18
Begin, Menachem: UNRWA, 45–46
Beirut: UNRWA, 65, 71–74, 81
Ben-Porat, Mordechai: resettlement,
  109–10

Camp services officer: duties, 23–24,
  53
Camps: living conditions, 11, 51–53;
  leadership, 24;
  Six-Day War, 42;
  Lebanon, 63, 65, 67–68;
  Jordan, 89;
  Syria, 97;
  future of UNRWA, 111–13
Charters, Tony: RAOs, 30–31
Conflict resolution: UNRWA, 20

Damascus: PLO, 97
Diplomacy: Lebanon, 79;
  Syria, 99–100

Economics: intifada, 6;
  development, 36–38, 38–39;
  West Bank, 41–42;
  rations program, 56;
  Jordan, 85–86;
  Syria, 95, 97, 103–104;

Palestinian state, 114, 116
Education: UNRWA priorities,
  11–12, 15–16, 54–55;
  textbooks, 55;
  Lebanon, 66;
  Jordan, 90;
  teachers, 90, 98;
  Syria, 103
Egypt: refugees, 40–41

Finances, UNRWA: intifada, 19–20;
  population increase, 51;
  United States, 59–61;
  Syria, 102–105

Geneva Convention: Israel, 14, 46
General Authority for Palestine Arab
  Refugees (GAPAR): UNRWA,
  99–100, 102–104
Giacomelli, Giorgio: politics, 9–11;
  Israelis and intifada, 13–14;
  peace process, 61–62;
  future of UNRWA, 118, 119–20
Griffith, John: RAOs, 21–22

Health services: UNRWA, 11, 15,
  18–20
Hizballah: kidnappings, 76
Housing: Lebanon, 66–68;
  Israel, 110, 111;
  West Bank and Gaza, 114
Humanitarian assistance: UNRWA,
  9, 10

Information: Israelis and UNRWA,
  13;
  RAOs and shebab, 26
Institutions: UNRWA and Syria, 102;
  future of UNRWA, 117
Intifada: health services, 18–19;
  community life, 19;
  UNRWA finances, 19–20;
  camp leadership, 24–26;
  PLO, 25–26;

Jordan, 91;
resettlement, 111;
UNRWA and Israel, 113
Israel: invasion of Lebanon, 4–5;
UNRWA and government, 12, 16,
43–45;
United Nations and refugees, 33,
34;
West Bank and Gaza, 41;
Six-Day War, 43;
future of UNRWA, 109–11;
See also Army, Israeli

Jahr, Karin: RAOs, 27, 28, 29
de Jonge, Franke: UNRWA and
Lebanon, 74–75, 77–81
Jordan: Palestinian refugees, 40;
rations program, 57, 58

Kidnapping: Lebanon, 75–76

Michelmore, Laurence: UNRWA and
Six-Day War, 40–41
Mills, Bernard: UNRWA and Israelis,
17
Morale: West Bank and Gaza, 6;
UNRWA and Syria, 100
Mukhtars: camp leadership, 24

Nashashibi, Muhammad: Syria, 95,
97–98, 106;
future of UNRWA, 113–15
Nationalism: Six-Day War, 42–43;
Jordan, 89–91

Palestine Liberation Organization
(PLO): United States, 5;
intifada leadership, 25–26;
Lebanon, 68–71;
Jordan, 87–88, 92;
Syria, 97, 101–102;
future of UNRWA, 114;
Palestinian state, 115, 119
Perez de Cuellar, Javier: intifada, 14;
UNRWA policies, 14–15
Politics: UNRWA, 9–10;
Jordan, 86, 92–94;
Syria, 97–98
Population: increase, 42, 50–51;
Jordan, 83;
UNRWA statistics, 115

Qalandiyya camp: RAOs and Israeli
army, 30–31

Rafah camp: living conditions, 52–53
Rations program: UNRWA policy,
55–57, 58;
Lebanon, 65–66;
Jordan, 85;
Syria, 104–105
Refugee Affairs Officer (RAO):
UNRWA, 20–24, 26–27, 29–31;
women, 27–28
Refugees: United Nations, 32–33;
definition, 48–49;
Lebanon, 67
Registration: system, 49–50
Repatriation: United Nations, 34–35;
economic development, 36–38, 39
Resettlement: Israeli policy, 109–11

Security: camps, 54;
Lebanon, 74–75, 76–80;
Syria, 98–99, 100–101
Self-government: Palestinian
leadership, 108–109
Sha'ath, Nabil: future of UNRWA,
115–17
Shatila camp: refugees in Lebanon,
72–73
Shebab: intifada, 24–25;
RAOs and information, 26
Shufat camp: RAOs, 28–30
Siblin: UNRWA and PLO, 69, 80–82
Six-Day War: UNRWA, 40
Syria: rations program, 57;
PLO and Beirut, 73

United Nations: secretary-general's
report on intifada, 13–15;
future of UNRWA, 107, 118–19
United Nations' Children's Fund
(UNICEF): intifada, 20
United States: PLO, 5;
UN veto, 15;
UNRWA finances, 59–61, 69

Vienna: UNRWA headquarters, 48

West Bank: army and schools, 15–16;
Six-Day War, 40;
Jordan, 92–93

Yarmouk: Palestinians in Syria, 95;
demonstrations, 101

Zach, Fredy: future of UNRWA, 111